Communication for Consultants

Communication for Consultants

Rita R. Owens
Carroll School of Management,
Boston College

BEP BUSINESS EXPERT PRESS

Communication for Consultants

First published in 2016 by
Business Expert Press, LLC
222 East 46th Street, New York, NY 10017
www.businessexpertpress.com

ISBN-13: 978-1-63157-377-4 (paperback)
ISBN-13: 978-1-63157-378-1 (e-book)

Business Expert Press Corporate Communication Collection

Collection ISSN: 2156-8162 (print)
Collection ISSN: 2156-8170 (electronic)

Cover and interior design by Exeter Premedia Services Private Ltd., Chennai, India

First edition: 2016

10 9 8 7 6 5 4 3 2 1

Printed in the United States of America.

Dave and Andy, my two great consultants

Abstract

From the moment of their first client engagement, consultants in all fields face communication opportunities and challenges. No matter what their focus may be—professional services, accounting, technology, operations, human resources, manufacturing, or marketing—consultants drive change. That change, from its initial definition through its development and deployment, must be precisely communicated to a variety of audiences and through a variety of mediums.

Most business communication books do a good job leading professional writers and presenters through the basics of audience, organization, formatting, and mechanics. But, only few focus on a specific business role, such as that of a consultant, and give guidance for communicating during all stages of a project. From the pre-engagement process, to the actual engagement, to the post-engagement follow-up, consultants are challenged by the variety of audiences whose roles continually shift throughout a project.

This book guides a current or would-be consultant through the various phases of a typical engagement and gives practical advice and direction on written and oral communication throughout a project. Current and future consultants in all fields will gain specific knowledge about writing and presenting to a variety of audiences including clients, team members, managers, and executives.

Keywords

business communication, business correspondence, business etiquette, business writing, consulting, e-mails, engagements, meetings, presentations, proposals, reports

Contents

Disclaimer..xi

Preface xiii

Acknowledgments...xv

Introduction xvii

Chapter 1   Key Considerations for Consultants....................1

Chapter 2   Pre-Engagement Communication.....................15

Chapter 3   Engagement Communication 49

Chapter 4   Post-Engagement Communication 91

Appendix A 107

Appendix B 111

Notes..113

References 115

Index 117

Disclaimer

All persons, places, projects, and companies appearing in this work are fictitious. Any resemblance to real persons or entities, living or dead, is purely coincidental.

Preface

I've wanted to write this book for many years. It's a combination of my experiences as a consultant and as a business communication instructor. Having been an external and internal consultant in several organizations, I've always been fascinated with the client–consultant relationship and how it manifests through communication. When I was a new consultant years ago, I had little advance knowledge or direction about how I should communicate with my clients. I was young and thought I could conquer the world. Fortunately, I had good common sense, but I also made my share of mistakes. Sometimes I said or wrote too little; most of the time I said too much. I always wished I had a book to help me bridge the communication gaps between my customer and me. This is that book.

I've written this book for those of you who call yourselves consultants or are about to become one. You come in many flavors. Some of you are management consultants. Many of you are internal consultants challenged by interdepartmental exchanges. Others are business analysts overseeing implementations at client sites. You work for large firms and small companies. Many of you work for yourselves. What you share is the incredible challenge of helping a client advance. I hope this books helps you succeed and that your excellent communications lead the way.

Acknowledgments

Thanks to my family and friends who continually support me in all I do. I am very appreciative of the many consultants and clients who shared their insights, stories, and advice over the course of this project. Special thanks go to the Boston College Carroll School of Management for welcoming me and especially to Dean Andy Boynton whose focus on teaching excellence has made a significant impact on my career. I also happily acknowledge my Boston College business communication students; their intelligence and curiosity energize me every day.

I owe the book's outcome to many but especially to Debbie DuFrene, my patient editor, and to Rosie Gonzalez, my research assistant. For her expert review, guidance, and encouragement, I am beyond grateful to Professor Mary Cronin of Boston College. Many thanks to Lisa Bruni and Cristina Mirshekari, great colleagues and friends, who so generously reviewed my work and gave me spot-on feedback.

Finally, I want to acknowledge the late Dr. Frank B. Campanella, my amazing mentor. His legacy continues to inspire and motivate me.

Introduction

Why This Book?

Consultants in any practice need excellent communication skills or they will fail. There is no question that the most important skill for a consultant is to be able to communicate clearly and effectively. Of course, it is important to be able to manage people and projects, to be able to oversee technology and its implementation, and to drive change, but success with any of these is based on solid communication. The goal of this book is to help consultants and would-be consultants focus on effective communication methodologies that support their own success and that of their clients.

The very nature of being a consultant puts us in the role of an expert. As a consultant we take on the role of someone whom others look to. We give advice, we give direction, we give approval, we make change, we correct problems, we forge new direction, we alter the past, and we make way for the future. In some respects, we set ourselves up to be people whom others want to emulate. We are in the position to sell services, projects, and ideas; we lead projects, troubleshoot, mediate, manage, and direct. Our roles are so diverse, and we balance all of this interaction with both internal and external clients and colleagues. The only way to meet these varied expectations is through excellent business communication.

Of course, we all know that much of a consultant's output is in writing or oral presentations, and this output is exactly what the client is paying us for. We produce the blueprint. That is our product. It needs to be accurate, clear, and precise. And while this might sound obvious, it is often overlooked as a priority because of our competing demands during an engagement. Beyond this, intercultural and remote communications have increased our challenges exponentially; so, we should carefully reflect on our skills.

The key characteristic of excellent business writing is to focus on the relationship with the audience and its needs. Yet, in a consulting situation, that audience role and relationship continues to change and morph as a project develops. For example, the manager to whom we may initially sell consulting services might become the key partner with whom we work very closely to mobilize our own team and perhaps that of the manager. So, we first walk in as a stranger and very quickly turn into the colleague, yet this does not change our relationship with the people to whom we are writing or presenting. Relationships are a key area we explore in this text.

Most great consultants are successful not only because they are talented and insightful but also because they use good judgment. They know how to manage professional relationships, be discreet, and still be collegial with a client. The knack of balancing multiple roles throughout an engagement and being able to communicate professionally is tricky and deserves our careful examination.

Audience needs dictate our communication. They control our tone, our format, the length of our piece, what information we include and exclude, what medium we use, and even how we send or deliver our message. In this text we explore a variety of business communication strategies and outputs that we typically develop for our clients during an engagement's lifecycle. We do this with an eye on the shifting relationship with our audience and how it controls and influences what we write and present.

Who Will Benefit from This Book?

Whether you are already consulting and stepping inside of someone else's territory or aspiring to do that, this book is for you. It provides information and methodology to help you become more successful as an independent consultant or as a consultant working for a large firm. The material is also relevant for professionals who have an internal consulting role within their company or institution. Whether you're in school and considering a consulting career or you've been consulting for many years, the information and methodology here will help you become more successful.

Much of what we discuss applies to all professional workplace communication. However, this book especially focuses on those engagements where we enter a client's workspace in a very intimate way and become part of that client's family. We will explore ways to avoid pitfalls and to deliver an effective, clear, and appropriate message throughout an engagement.

In school we learn to write or present for one audience—a teacher or professor. Of course that person knows our material, sometimes even better than we do. We rarely learn to write to a client, employee, or senior manager, let alone to one of these with a particular need related to what we have to say. That might include, for example, the disgruntled client, the employee we're trying to retain, or the misinformed senior manager. Yet, as consultants these varying client situations make up the audiences with whom we must communicate in order to succeed.

What's in the Book?

You will find much practical advice for someone beginning a consulting career or brushing up after many engagements. The book covers a variety of communication forms, but especially those in written form. It provides scenarios and examples organized around communication challenges that you're likely to encounter before, during, and after an engagement. We will dissect standard professional services engagements and their deliverables as consultants encounter them. And we will look at many of the deliverables and provide practical examples for those who consult. We will explore business communication with the unique view of the shifting client relationship throughout the pre-engagement, engagement, and post-engagement phases.

CHAPTER 1

Key Considerations for Consultants

You and Your Audience

The Uniqueness of Communicating as a Consultant

When we enter a new consulting engagement, our audience—our client, welcomes us; but there is also natural tension in this relationship. Our clients or key stakeholders are the internals and we are the externals, the consultants. As mentioned in the introduction of this text, the relationship among consultants and clients evolves over time. We hope this happens in a positive way, but sometimes it does not. How does communication impact our relationship development? Well, communication is literally "our word" and the client will go back to that word over and over again. In the best scenario we go back to documentation to ensure that the work after an engagement follows the original mission or vision. In the worst scenario, the documentation becomes the detail that we may dispute once the engagement is over.

Effective communication is important throughout business. It's the basis upon which we conduct business. We don't communicate for entertainment or self-aggrandizement. For consultants, exceptional communication must be the standard. Anything a consultant writes or presents becomes part of the contract deliverable. It determines whether a relationship, a project, or an engagement succeeds or fails. It is not to be taken lightly.

Recently I spoke to a partner at a large consulting firm, and he shared an example illustrating how communications can go especially wrong for a consultant. He related a story about a small team working with a client and that client's sudden dissatisfaction with the project.

Seemingly out of nowhere, the senior consulting manager on the project received a scathing e-mail from the client expressing that the team was not capable of carrying out the tasks at hand. The client felt that the team was too junior and not well equipped. The senior manager and his partner decided the best course of action would be to meet with the client face to face. When they did, they learned that the client really wasn't unhappy with the team's work but actually with its communication. The client felt that the team was driving to recommendations without including him and was actually sidestepping him. He felt the project was heading in a direction that sought to destroy the department he had created. As it turned out, the analyst in charge of the project team was so keen to complete the documentation and design work required to move the project forward that he and his team simply forgot to slow down and include the client in their communication.[1]

This example serves to emphasize the critical problem of consultant/client miscommunication. As consultants we are often completely driven to produce the final deliverable and often with the best of intentions. Our work is billable, and we want to be as efficient as possible. It's easy for us to forget that there are other people in the mix, particularly our clients.

Two critical communication-related issues emerge from the preceding example. First, the consulting executives had the sense to know that replying to the e-mail would not really get to the heart of the problem, and perhaps an informal approach would even inflame the situation. They knew that a face-to-face meeting, rather than a quick e-mail reply, was necessary to understand what was actually going on. Second, the executives knew that the complaints in the e-mail might not represent the issue at hand. In the meeting, they learned that the client actually felt alienated from the project.

Let's review the two takeaways from the example and how they connect to this uniqueness of communication within consulting:

1. Keep your audience (your clients) foremost in mind when working and communicating with them. The absence of communication is as significant as what you actually write and present.

2. Be very deliberate about using appropriate mediums, especially when handling a difficult situation. Don't write or call when you need to meet.

What Characterizes the Consulting Role and Why Exceptional Communication Is So Important

As consultants, we produce deliverables that are reviewed and considered expert. Most of the time these deliverables are in the form of written communication, which is followed by or preceded by oral communication. The bottom line is that our output can be a piece of communication. Often, the product in consulting is our intellectual capital expressed in a communication. For example, when we complete an organizational redesign we offer a written plan with recommendations for implementation. Of course, a good plan or analysis helps a client actually implement that new organization, but the plan itself is what the consultant creates and delivers. In essence, it's what our client is buying. And these plans we produce, whether they are multiple-page documents or PowerPoint presentations, become permanent artifacts for the client. Long after the consultant is gone the artifact lives on, and it often becomes the basis of a client's strategic vision.

Our communication must be clear. It must meet its objectives. It must stand the test of time. It must be logical. More than anything, it must be audience-focused.

Consultant Communication General Assumptions and Guidelines

Communicating as a consultant demands rigorous attention to detail and a commitment to excellent business writing and presentation standards.

Polished Professional Delivery

As noted above, our communication is our product so it must be as close to perfect as we can achieve. Frankly there is no room for error when a consultant communicates.

Many years ago, a technology consultant told a story that stuck with me. This particular consultant was just about to close on a very important contract. In the final stages of the negotiations, when things were going very well and it appeared that the consultant would seal the deal, one small error made a tremendous difference in the outcome. This small business consultant had been able to win the deal over some very large competing companies. He had been able to overcome the typical obstacles of representing a small business. A polished orator, the consultant was able to convince the client that his small company would do the best job.

A final meeting was organized, and the night before the meeting the consultant hastily wrote some product sheets to solidify what would be delivered. The next morning at the meeting, the client appeared and surprisingly announced he had decided not to enter into the contract. As it turned out, he had read those final product briefs the night before and found a spelling error. The word "successfully" had been misspelled multiple times. All the client's fears about working with a small company came to bear upon his final decision. His last words to the consultant were, "We thought, what kind of a person would we be dealing with if he can't spell simple words?"

Of course, years later in our world with spellchecking tools we can't imagine spelling prohibiting our success. However, it's very easy to overlook critical editing especially when we're multitasking and responding too quickly; and it's important to know that it matters.

General Assumptions

Before we begin to analyze our writing, let's review some overall general assumptions and guidelines relevant to consultant writing and presenting:

- Consultants communicate to conduct business. That is the overarching reason for our communication. We don't communicate to show what we know, but we communicate to respond to the client audience needs at a particular moment in time.
- Consultant communication is very different from the kind of communication we write personally or in school. Our tone,

our language, what we include, what we exclude, and more are completely determined by the value proposition for the audience, the client.

- The essence of consultant communications is relationship building. We must choose the appropriate medium, depending on the situation and the client's needs.
- Consultant communication is part of the permanent record of activities between a consultant and the client. It must be created and produced at the highest professional level possible.
- Consultants typically communicate within a specified time period and often with a firm deadline. Consultant communication is either written or presented, typically under much pressure of time or circumstance. This pressure puts us at increased risk of producing unrefined communication, but we must do everything we can to avoid that.
- The success of a project depends on excellent communication; therefore our communication is critical and costly.
- Consultant communication often follows a template or a particular protocol. Many large corporations minimize their risk of communication problems by providing a template, but great consultants are equipped to go it alone.
- Consultant communication might be facilitated in a classic style or in a contemporary mode. All consultants should be proficient in English usage and traditional models, but we must also be adept with modern social media and digital communication options.
- Consultant communication is professional in appearance, format, and style.
- At all times, and in all communication, we must approach our client with great consideration and respect. The best way to ensure this happens is to consider all communication as an integral part of conducting business. Too often, our written communications and our presentations are afterthoughts. They often follow the "real" work we have done, so we don't consider them critical to our success. Nothing could be further from the truth.

But beyond having well formatted, grammatically correct materials, what should our communications entail? Let's review the attributes, mediums, and techniques commonly found in good business communication.

What It Sounds Like

There is a particular tone to a business letter or presentation. After all, we are conducting business, not writing or presenting creative material. Often, we presume that if we're writing or presenting on an important matter that we must take on an air of sophistication and intellectualism. We think our sentences and vocabulary must sound academic because of the nature of the topic. Actually, the reality is quite the opposite. Business communication is the byproduct of conducting business; it is not itself the business. So we must focus on presenting clearly, even if that means we are more blunt than we're typically comfortable being.

Consider these characteristics of good consulting communication:

Messages are sharp, crisp, and to the point
Not This: After much analysis, we are requesting that you consider changing your business practices to allow for more advanced customer relations management technology.
But This: We recommend you purchase a customer relations management system.

Messages are precise
Not This: There are a lot of problems with the current e-mail server that must be addressed.
But This: We have found seven e-mail server issues that need attention.

Sentences are in the active voice
Not This: Final reports will be distributed to the clients by the consulting team.
But This: The consulting team will distribute final reports to the clients.

Language is professional
Not This: We're kind of worried about a lot of the accounting practices we've found.
But This: We have some concerns about many of the accounting practices we have encountered.

What It Looks Like

Beyond using an appropriate style and tone, choosing the right communication medium and format is important. We determine what medium and format we use based on our purpose, the audience's disposition, and the circumstances surrounding the communication. We'll review this when we develop our audience analysis later in this chapter. But to give you a general sense of what business communication looks like, let's review the following:

- Established business protocols can determine the "look." Formal business letters, memoranda, e-mails, texts, slide presentations, face-to-face meetings, and virtual meetings each prescribe a particular approach.
- Sentences tend to be short and direct. Paragraphs are short, too, and they are typically left justified, single spaced, with double spacing in between.
- Charts, graphs, and other visuals complement text.
- Headings are used to guide the audience toward particular topics.
- Bullet points are used to make the material easily read and digestible.

The Communication Creation Process

In all our communication we must be acutely aware of our audience; our goal is to make comprehension easy for the reader or listener. People can't afford to waste time unnecessarily on reading and meeting, so writing and presenting must be succinct, clear, and to the point. In other words, we must be time and effort conscious.

Electronic delivery of materials, via e-mail especially, has eroded many of our established business communication standards. Of course, we all embrace the ability to communicate rapidly with one another, but this immediate interaction does create challenges. For example, before e-mail, we would craft a report or proposal on paper and it would be delivered with the daily mail. Our client might set aside time to read that mail and give the report or proposal and all its elements his or her full attention.

Today, many of our executive clients average 100 or more e-mails per day; the management of the inbox in itself has become a chore. So, when we attach large reports to those e-mails, they can easily be overlooked or ignored. Because of the technology shift, it has become increasingly more important to choose the appropriate medium and format when communicating. We can no longer take for granted that our client has the luxury of time to read lengthy documents.

Howard Weinberg, retired principal at Deloitte Consulting, recently gave me some great advice on this matter. When discussing his concerns about consultant communications, he cited the problems that result when we focus on our own interests rather than on those of the audience. When I asked Mr. Weinberg what his greatest pet peeve was about business communicators, here's what he said:

> Not thinking through the value to the audience—why is this a really good use of their time? Functional value (what can they do with the information), social value (others see them as important because they are involved/informed), emotional (learn something new that's valuable/interesting). Like the real estate rule about "location, location, location" it is about "value, value, value" of each element of the communication for the audience. Just because you are proud of it, think it's cool, or it is a fact about our project is no reason to communicate it.[2]

The best way to ensure that our communication is audience-focused is to begin with an analysis of audience needs and how to provide that "value, value, value."

Audience Analysis Methodology

Whenever we write or present, we assume that our letter, memo, e-mail, report, proposal, or slide presentation will be read or heard. However, this isn't a realistic assumption since we are not in control of our audience and in no way can predict whether they will actually read or understand what we've presented to them. The best way to increase our chances of being heard is to put ourselves in our audience's shoes and craft our communication from their perspective. We are usually quite fixated on what we want to say, but we need to be more focused on what the audience needs to hear.

Audience Analysis: Responding to Messages and Queues

To ensure our communication is successful, we should pause for 10 seconds, or at times 10 minutes, and conduct an audience analysis that will guide our communication. But most of us don't think to do this. Interestingly, we're usually quite skilled at outlining our communication because we are taught that in school. But if you think about it, our obsession to outline well is a result of our interest in presenting what we know, not necessarily what our audience needs. We are typically so caught up in saying or writing something that we forget why we're even doing that and how it will be received. In essence, this is the crux of why audience analysis is so important. All of the decisions we make about our communication flow from our audience's perspective.

Traditionally, business communication guidelines advise us to focus on audience analysis by identifying and determining some situational elements in advance of our written or spoken output. We might, for example, decide what tone we should write in and what format we should employ. But when working as a consultant, it is so critical to accurately assess a client's needs that we must consider a wide range of audience particulars to help guide our communication.

Situation > Product > Delivery

At the highest level, three elements control audience analysis in consultancy communication. Before we prepare our communication, it's critical that we analyze the conditions surrounding our audience analysis so we can best interact with our client. We must identify the *situation* we find ourselves and our client in, which will lead us to the output, or *product*, we will produce, which will direct us to the medium, or *delivery* we will use. This may seem like a daunting task, but taking a few minutes to scope out communication gives us the confidence that we will produce excellent output.

Here are the overall conditions you should consider as you prepare your communications.

> *Situation*: Value, Purpose, Message, Directive, Relationship, Climate and Culture, Deadline
> *Product*: Wrapper, Content, Organization, Tone, Language, Length
> *Delivery*: Virtual (e-mail, text), Physical (paper), Meeting, Multiple

Let's review these three major condition criteria for client audience analysis, their supporting details, and interdependencies.

Situation

This is the most critical of the three criteria because it is the situation we find ourselves in that directs and motivates us to communicate in the first place. When we evaluate *situation* we pay particular attention to our client's needs and our own. We also survey the environment surrounding our communication to determine the conditions under which we are creating it. As you scope *situation*, consider the following:

- **Value**: What does this client want or need from your communication? What's the value to him/her/them? Is this an engagement-critical matter or an everyday matter? Does the audience have the time or motivation to devote to this communication in the way you present it? *Value* to the client is why we write or present. Put yourself in this person's place and understand what he or she needs and wants from the communication.
- **Purpose**: Why have you actually chosen to communicate? What do you want or need out of this? Are you inquiring, applying, informing, reporting, proposing, rejecting, or denying? *Purpose* often relates to specific protocols in business communication.
- **Message**: What kind of message are you transmitting? Good news? Bad news? *Message* directly relates to your tone and, in some cases, to protocols surrounding how a piece is organized.
- **Directive**: Has the client asked for this, or have you just decided to communicate on your own? Are you being reactive

or proactive to a situation? The *directive* controls how much you might include and exclude as background.

- **Relationship**: What is your relationship with the reader? Is she a partner at the client site? Is she your internal team leader? And what is that person's predisposition to the topic? Is the audience neutral, nervous, or excited about the topic? Have there been any volatile matters between you and the client preceding this communication? *Relationship* can drive tone, content, format, language, and delivery.

- **Climate and Culture**: Are there methods and modes of communication at the client site that you should be aware of? Will your communication create problems at the client site? Should you adjust your typical mode of communication to suit the client culture? *Climate and culture* have an impact on what you include and exclude as well as whom you even choose to receive your communication.

- **Deadline**: When does the communication need to reach the client in order for it to be effective? What is the best time to send this communication? Is there an actual deadline for this within the project plan? *Deadline* drives when you must complete the communication. It can also influence what the best time is to actually communicate.

Product

Once you've considered those elements in *situation*, the actual *product* you'll produce becomes much clearer. You know what both your client and you need from the communication, so you're now prepared to think through what the actual communication will look like, what it will include or exclude, what it will sound like, how it will be organized, and how long it will be.

You should now be ready to make decisions involving the following:

- **Wrapper**: What's the best way to actually wrap the communication? Should you write a memorandum, a business letter, a freestanding report? Is there a template the client prefers? Should you communicate this in person at a client meeting, or is sending an e-mail update sufficient and preferred? Depending on the situation, you should be able to determine the preferred *wrapper*.

- **Content**: Depending on the *purpose* and *value*, you can now determine what your content should be. Of course, content depends very much on the particular business at hand. Generally speaking, however, the *situation* should help guide you as you construct your content. How much detail should you include based on the *situation*? Does the content add *value* for the client? Is your purpose clear based on the *content*? Do you handle the *relationship* appropriately? Does the treatment of content mirror the client's *culture and climate*?

- **Organization**: Regardless of the *wrapper* you choose, you must decide which method of organization to use. Should you present your ideas from the least to the most important or most important to least importance? Does it make more sense to organize sequentially or chronologically? The *situation*, most importantly *value* and *purpose*, contribute significantly to this decision.

- **Tone**: How you sound in client communication is so important. Do you want to come across as confident? Careful? Considerate? Authoritative? Demanding? Conciliatory? Reflecting on *situation* should guide your tone.

- **Language**: Similar to tone, the language you use is directly related to the *relationship* you have with the client and the *climate and culture* you find yourself in. Should your language be formal or informal? Does the audience understand the type of language you are using? Are you writing or presenting in the active voice so you're best understood?

- **Length**: The *situation* should also inform the length of the communication. This may seem obvious, but it isn't always. You want to write as much as the *situation* warrants, no more or less. Just because you have a great deal of information on a topic doesn't mean you should write or present it all. Be acutely aware of the *value* to the client. Is this a two- to three-paragraph written piece? Can you best make your case in under 10 slides?

Delivery

By this point, you've defined and made preliminary decisions about the characteristics of the product. Now you can address the actual delivery mechanism you will use to communicate your message. Consider the following delivery modes and their idiosyncrasies:

- **Virtual**: Most of what we transact these days is delivered via e-mail or text messages. But is the *wrapper* you've selected easily read within an e-mail on a mobile or computer device? Does the *situation* call for a piece that needs special formatting, visuals, or other elements not conducive to online viewing? Should the piece be attached to the e-mail in a mode that ensures formatting will stay intact? Is online viewing actually preferred because you've included video, links to websites, and other electronic materials? Is the conversational flow of text messages appropriate for a professional communication? *Situation* should guide you in these decisions, especially as it relates to *value* and *climate and culture.*

- **Physical**: Sometimes the best mode of delivery is still paper. This doesn't necessarily mean you send a paper report via a postal service, but it does mean that the best way to communicate is for someone to read a written document. You often need a written document if you want a physical signature on a communication. More often, however, you may want special design elements to be in place that are not conducive to reading on a screen. Beyond these practicalities, some clients still have a *climate and culture* that fosters paper documents. Answering these critical questions will help you identify the best delivery mode: How does your client transmit communications internally? Will your *wrapper* be best presented on paper? Even if you deliver your *product* via e-mail, can it be easily printed while retaining its format and distributed if the client chooses to do so?

- **Meeting**: You must also consider if a meeting is the best way to present your *product.* The *situation* will drive this more than anything. Is it more valuable to the client to receive this information in person, perhaps with an opportunity to discuss it immediately? Does a meeting guarantee that your *purpose* is more likely to be achieved? Should the meeting be face-to-face, technology assisted, one-on-one, or in a group? All of these decisions flow from situation and its various elements including *value, purpose, message, directive, relationship, climate and culture, and deadline.*

(For a summary of best practices in delivery modes, see Appendix B, Delivery Modes by Communication Type.)

Good audience analysis sets us up for communication success. As we've discussed, there are many elements to consider before we even begin to write or present. As consultants, every communication is critical to our success. It's critical to survey the landscape before we write or present. Once we've done that, we can confidently turn to the types of products and delivery modes we encounter in the pre-engagement, engagement, and post-engagement phases of a project.

CHAPTER 2

Pre-Engagement Communication

In this chapter, we will explore the first of three phases that make up a consulting engagement. The pre-engagement phase of a project typically runs from an initial inquiry through contract completion. In this chapter we will:

- review types of communication during this phase,
- detail the environment from both a consultant and a client's perspective,
- discuss good listening during pre-engagement phase, and
- illustrate best approaches to essential communications during this phase.

The Pre-Engagement Phase

While all consultants are directly involved in the engagement phase of a project, many contribute during the pre-engagement phase. This is especially true for small business consultants who manage all aspects of their client relationships. Whether actively involved in the communication or just by-standing, a consultant does well to know about all communication that will ultimately impact the actual engagement.

The pre-engagement phase is the period when your company introduces itself and begins to conduct business with a client. The relationship is established or re-kindled, and all parties seek to establish the ground rules for engagement. Most of your communication focuses on the documents and presentations necessary to start up the project. The communication tends to be more formal and detailed in this phase as everyone is learning how to interact with one another and to understand the work at hand.

The Pre-Engagement Communication

At this point, you as a consultant may not be responsible for much of your firm's communication with the client, but it's important that you have some insight into correspondence, contracts, and other deliverables your client receives. If you are part of a large consulting firm, those documents will likely be standard. If you work for a smaller consulting company or if you are an independent consultant, you will likely create these documents yourself. Regardless, be familiar with the background, detail, tone, and format of these communications, as you may want to mirror them during the engagement.

The pre-engagement phase can be thought of as a period of introduction, and much of the communication that takes place is a mega question-and-answer exercise. Most of the communication revolves around both parties becoming acquainted; so all interactions are, in essence, contractual. Matters of security and confidentiality surround much of the exchanges, so discretion is key. All communication now begins to form the documentation of an engagement, even if a contract has not yet been signed.

A significant amount of informal communication also occurs during pre-engagement phase. Sales staff and clients often spend a great deal of time together communicating on the phone, via e-mail, at lunches or dinners, and in small one-on-one meetings. While these interchanges are typically not recorded as official documentation, good ongoing dialog between your firm's sales and consulting arms can ensure continuity of message.

Later in this chapter we will review several materials you will likely create, but let's first look at the overall communication landscape during pre-engagement phase.

Preliminary Correspondence and Documentation

At the beginning of the relationship, there are a number of possible communications between your firm and the client. Those might include the following.

Letter of Inquiry: This business correspondence is written to gain more information about a company's particular offerings. Within the framework of consultant communication, a letter of inquiry is typically written by the prospective client to your firm inquiring about capacity to perform a particular job.

Sales Letter: This business correspondence is typically written by your sales personnel to a prospective client putting forth the value of doing business with your firm. In a large consulting firm, the sales team initiates these. If you're a small consulting business owner, you will write these letters as you develop your client base.

Requests for Information: Consultants don't write these messages to clients, but they do respond to them. Requests for Information (RFIs) are useful when a customer wants to know more about your services or products. An RFI may contain a simple request for general information, or it may actually ask for very detailed information. It's helpful to think about it this way: A client is shopping at this point, but not necessarily buying.

Requests for Proposals: Clients send Requests for Proposals (RFPs) when they are buying. An RFP is a solicitation for proposals, sometimes within a set bidding process. These documents typically detail all of the client's requirements concerning your services and products. As a consultant, you will not generally write these, but you may be asked to contribute information about your services and deliverables when your firm responds to the RFP. When responding to an RFP, your company will detail all deliverables, products, services, timelines, processes, and costs associated with a potential contract.

Product Specifications: Project managers and others often will record product and services specifications within other documents, such as RFPs, contracts, and implementation plans. These specifics detail a client's required product or services characteristics and are important to you as a consultant because they define what you or the firm must deliver during an engagement.

Proposal: When your company responds to an RFP or other official request, it puts forth a plan for potential clients to consider. Proposals are typically written formally and constitute the basis for a contract. A proposal typically includes the description of the plan, the benefits of it, any product specifications, the work schedule, the scope of work, and projected costs.

Agreements

Formal agreements can include a number of elements, with the most common ones described as follows.

Nondisclosure agreement: Clients often are asked to sign a nondisclosure agreement (NDA) during the pre-engagement period. An NDA is a contract between signing parties not to divulge particular information or knowledge about a business or its services.

Contract: This is the legally binding agreement between your firm and the client. It is typically a very formal document with specific details about responsibility and delivery that were first discussed in preliminary proposals.

Statement of Work: A Statement of Work (SOW) describes the deliverables you will provide during the engagement. The SOW typically details a schedule (including milestone deliverables), all activities, and responsible contributors to the work. It also may include costs associated with specific work, responsible paying parties, and the governance structure for decision making. The SOW can be used with internal or external clients to define a project; with external clients, it functions as the basis for the contract.

Project Plans: Project plans are usually delivered after a contract is signed but early in the engagement process, sometimes during pre-engagement phase. Project plans expand what is covered in the SOW. The project manager typically produces them and will include your consultant deliverables as part of that plan. A project plan usually includes overall mission statements, scope, roles and responsibilities, and activities. Good project plans also build in communication checkpoints or milestones, and often there is a separate, coordinated Communications Plan that's developed and agreed upon by both parties.

Meetings, Presentations, and Demonstrations

Besides written communication, there are a variety of in-person meetings and presentations that are documented during the period before the engagement. That documentation might include the following.

Meeting Minutes: Meeting minutes summarize the names of attendees, decisions, plans, motions, and new business discussed at a particular meeting session. It's important to track meetings by crafting accurate minutes, as they create the official record of all activities and provide an overview of actions that should be taken.

Project Introduction: During pre-engagement phase, lead consultants will usually introduce themselves, their team, and its roles and responsibilities to the clients. Likely this is the first of many presentations the consultant will make, but it's a critical one in that the team is creating a first impression and establishing the foundation for the working relationship.

Examples and tips for writing various types of pre-engagement communications are located at the end of this chapter.

The Pre-Engagement Environment

During this phase, you will typically write quite formally as most of the communication directly relates to contractual obligations. You are usually trying to put your best foot forward as you introduce yourself and set the tone for the engagement. It is also a period when many parties communicate and contribute to the overall start-up documentation, so scrutiny of written and oral communication is key.

Let's review the environmental conditions that influence your communication and guide your audience analysis.

What the Consultant Brings to the Environment

Before an engagement begins, the sales division within an organization primarily will coordinate communication with the client. While you, as a consultant, may not be directly involved with the customer, it is important to know what the sales team has promised and heard as a result of its interactions. During the selling phase, expectations are established on both sides, and the consultant who leads or works on the resulting project should have knowledge of any agreements.

The written and oral communication during this phase is typically carefully choreographed and involves many constituents with differing motivations. This is the "wooing period" when your sales staff eagerly develops the conditions for a signed contract. Communication is often formal and sometimes even prescribed by the company. After all, you are an outsider at this point. As the service provider, you want to ensure that there is no miscommunication about what you will deliver; so typically you will be very detailed in your approach. Company templates often are used to standardize what is presented to a client. Of course, your sales staff is eager to gain new business, so consultants sometimes find themselves operating under some vague principles that need further refinement as an engagement progresses. Bluntly put, a sales person may promise a deliverable that a consultant may have difficulty producing but that the client insists upon. There will be an opportunity to refine expectations, but be aware that a salesperson sees the environment very differently from a consultant delivering the service. Also, sales representatives typically enlist clients from previous engagements to recommend consulting services. This brings more writers into the mix with additional motivations.

How the Client Comes to the Environment

For your client, the pre-engagement phase is filled with many thoughts and emotions, which set the stage for the entire engagement. You must manage this process carefully through your communication, as these early exchanges set the tone for a positive, harmonious engagement or an adversarial, challenging one.

As we discussed previously, clients hire consultants to solve problems they typically cannot answer on their own or to validate what they theorize.[1]

These problems run the gambit from strategic positioning to reorganizing, to gaining efficiencies, to implementing a technology. You are called upon because of your unique expertise or because clients lack the time or knowledge to complete the project themselves. Projects are rarely straightforward, and their complex nature usually brings along many client assumptions, expectations, and emotions that impact everyone's communication. To better understand the client disposition during this phase, let's discuss the environment from their perspective.

Expectations and Assumptions

Within all projects, you will encounter the sponsors of the engagement, the clients who will work with you during the project, and the recipients of any disruption you will create. During the pre-engagement period, these three groups each typically bring distinct expectations and assumptions. It's important to be aware that some of your correspondence and presentations are simultaneously directed at these multiple audiences, each with differing attitudes toward the work.

For example, let's say you make a presentation during pre-engagement to scope the roles you will need on an implementation team. You may find yourself presenting to the project sponsors, department managers, and subject matter experts. In this early phase, each of these client representatives probably has very different expectations and assumptions about how the engagement will be managed and what the outcomes will be. The sponsor is probably confident that you can solve all the problems. The department manager might dread all the upheaval that's about to take place. The subject matter experts might be skeptical that you can deliver what you promise. So, while the expectations and assumptions can be wide and varied, the emotions behind these ideas are often even more volatile and significant—and more challenging to understand.

Negative Emotions and Attitudes

Change is hard. Whether you're the external consultant or the internal client on an important project, you approach the work with your own expectations, assumptions, emotions, and attitudes. These feelings can often permeate an engagement, especially during the pre-engagement period. It's important for a consultant to recognize the emotion during an engagement and demonstrate the professional demeanor in which everyone involved will operate. To be effective, it's also important to acknowledge what your clients may be experiencing and adjust your communication accordingly.

Because project startups stir much emotion, whether on the surface or as undercurrents, communicating directly and clearly is critical. Let's look at common emotions and attitudes during the pre-engagement period and evaluate how they might impact your communication:

- **Fear of Change or of the Unknown**: This is probably the most prevalent emotion surrounding an engagement but particularly during the start-up phase. No matter how well defined the engagement's mission and deliverables are, sponsors and managers usually have some trepidation and concern regarding what is about to happen. Even if everyone is in agreement that the change is for the better, it's likely they are unsure of the results and the accompanying effort necessary to achieve those. These fears require a consultant to be very consistent with all messages. Your writing must be direct and extremely intentional. For example, you should use the same words over and again when referring to the type of work you will do. Any new language you introduce can exacerbate the situation and create more fears.

- **Skepticism**: Don't be surprised to find a skeptical attitude accompanying the fear of change. In fact, almost everyone is a skeptic at this point in the project, except, of course, you. Many around you will prefer to keep doing work the way it has always been done and doubt that any changes you drive will indeed matter. That's what makes communication difficult. You have likely promised to make significant and considerable improvements, and many with whom you communicate might question if these will happen. Your communication, written or oral, must be balanced and concrete. This is not the time to sound as though you're overpromising, but you do want to come across as confident and clear.

- **Mistrust**: Along with skepticism comes mistrust. It's critical that all communication is forthright and precise during this period. Throughout an engagement, you may encounter the doubters who mistrust consultants. This makes it difficult for those of us, even with the purest of intentions, to be completely open for fear of appearing untrustworthy if we need to adjust our priorities as we move through a project. Again, your communication is under scrutiny during this stage of the project, so clear and reasonable articulation of goals and deliverables is critical.

- **Avoidance**: Many clients want to avoid the inevitable change that's about to be carried out. Even with project plans and team assignments in hand, many of those you'll work with will try to avoid what's coming. You may encounter client team members who hope you and your project will disappear. This is where great communicators have the advantage. When you make a conscious effort to communicate in open and informative ways with your new partners, you bring them closer to the work at hand by engaging them, thus moving the work forward.

- **Lack of Understanding**: There's a good chance that some of the people with whom you work won't understand why you've been contracted and what you'll deliver. You can't assume your project sponsors have been clear about deliverables, processes, or outcomes. It's your job as a consultant to work through any misunderstandings and ineffective interpretations about the engagement. You must be diplomatic and discreet, and your communication tactics and methods must be at their peak.

- **Anxiety**: Along with fear of the unknown, your clients can often carry anxiety about the change and the work involved. We all know that anxious people don't always absorb information well. They sometimes hear what they want to hear. This creates challenges for consultants because we need to gauge how hard to push and how much to say and when. Anxiety can be especially acute in the engagement start-up period when there is a certain amount of understandable confusion about roles, timeline, responsibilities, and more. It takes a skillful communicator to nip this anxiety in the bud before it permeates and hinders productivity throughout the full engagement.

- **Impatience**: Rarely does a client initiate a project without some urgency about its completion. After all, the customer has probably secured funding and resources for the project with some challenges. Those in charge want to move ahead quickly. You, too, probably feel some pressure to begin a project. Your own work schedule and resource allocation may demand that you move quickly. Additionally, many projects have a shelf life. They can be perishable in that failure to complete them on time negates their effectiveness or even their reason for being. It's no wonder many of a project's players are impatient. But overeager parties on either side can create serious communication problems. Communication can be lost or minimized when we're impatient, and we may not adequately manage critical information. This is not a symptom just during pre-engagement, as there are also many impatient parties throughout an engagement. However, from the beginning of a project, we must ensure that impatience never outweighs how and what we must communicate to ensure a positive outcome.

• **Resentment**: Members of the client team sometimes resent a consultant coming in to solve a problem or to give advice. Even though the client executives want the outside input, the internal subject matter experts may feel that hiring a consultant demeans their own internal roles and questions their abilities. This situation makes it extremely important for a consultant to communicate openly to build goodwill and foster cooperation.

Multiple Audiences and Multiple Representatives

Beyond the complicating factors we have just reviewed, a number of overarching audience considerations must be addressed within the pre-engagement phase. While some of these are not exclusive to pre-engagement phase, many are uniquely critical to this stage and each of those is important to understand as we define the environment.

Multiple Audiences

Much of a consultant's communication addresses multiple audiences throughout an engagement simply because there are typically many colleagues and clients involved throughout the process. However, during the pre-engagement process you are likely to encounter audiences with more widely varying interests than you will once the actual engagement begins. As projects begin, we often cast a wider net for our audience participation, and this implicitly generates complications for our communication. Further, at this point, these multiple audiences may have discrepant and possibly competing interests that must be understood by the consultant.

For example, let's say you are designing an introduction presentation that you'll deliver at a project kickoff meeting. You know that the project executives, sponsors, target directors, and managers will all be in the room. As you identify each of these audience types, you should consider what to include and exclude based on the various interests of all of these parties. In this case, the project sponsors probably understand best what's about to transpire and may have actually instigated the engagement. They are filled with ideas, possibilities, and expectations. The target directors and managers probably know fewer details and will come to the presentation with more apprehension and less knowledge than the sponsors.

As the engagement moves ahead, communications are directed at more focused audiences with more similar characteristics. But during pre-engagement, a consultant must pay attention to this multiple audience situation.

Multiple Representatives

Before an engagement begins, a consultant, even if already assigned to the particular project, might actually be on the sidelines of the initial activity. Until the contract is executed, an account manager may be your firm's key client representative, not you. It's worth noting that no matter how intentional your firm is to communicate clearly the engagement goals, processes, and deliverables, differing representative motivations might bring on differing messages. It's possible for you as the consultant to enter an engagement with project expectations that are quite different from those account executives described during the sales process. That can spell disaster for a consultant and a client. As much as possible, you should be involved in pre-engagement communications or at least be well aware of their specifics.

It's also worth mentioning that there are times throughout an engagement when no one on the consulting side should deliver a message regarding the project. In critical and delicate matters, the client should instead deliver the communication to the client's own staff.

At some point during the pre-engagement phase, probably toward the end of it when the contract is close to being signed, you will begin to communicate with the client. To overcome the awkwardness during this transitional period, mirror previous communications. Use similar templates, key messages, language, and tone to ensure continuity and clarity.

Listening During All Engagement Phases

Senior consulting executives often expect that a consultant must develop and master expert listening skills. During the pre-engagement period, careful listening not only allows a consultant to appear open to what a client is saying but also gives the consultant an opportunity to gain insight into issues that might arise during the engagement.

As we discussed in Chapter 1, consultants are considered experts and this assumption carries with it quite a bit of responsibility. To be a good consultant, you must be able to lead people toward new ideas and change. Unfortunately, problems can arise in the process. Many consultants think that the more they say, the smarter they look. And consultants like to look smart.[2] You are, in fact, under pressure to do just that. But talking over a client or presenting too much knowledge in advance of deeply considering a client's situation is a big mistake. It can create an immediate disconnect between you and the client, but more seriously, it can stop you from hearing what you must know to be productive and achieve desired results for the client and yourself. A better way to look smart is to facilitate an environment where everyone can share information in a nonthreatening, nonjudgmental manner. It's not difficult to do this, but it does take some awareness.

Much has been written on active listening, especially as it relates to the social sciences. In business, human resource specialists are well versed in this area. But consultants often overlook the very basic listening skills that can help them and their clients.

How to Listen

Experts on active listening tell us that a few simple strategies can create the exchange we are seeking. Here are some tips to help you:

- *Be present*: It might seem obvious, but the best way to listen is to be fixated on what is being said. Listen to every detail. Abandon distracting electronic devices. Don't try to think about your response too far in advance. Pay attention to what the client says and how she says it. Is there emotion? Is there concern? Catalog what you learn for further study and application in your communications.
- *Be open-minded*: Now is not the time to prove you are the expert. Don't assume the client doesn't know anything, even if it's concerning the very thing in which you consider yourself expert. Listen for those elements that will play out within the engagement, but don't necessarily feel compelled at this point to solve problems or reassure the client. Just take it all in.
- *Record the dialog*: While it can be awkward to record a discussion, it might work in a large group setting when you want to capture all that is being said. Ask permission to do so. This record will allow you to review the intricacies of what the client is saying, and you'll hear it more clearly after the fact. If you can't record, take as many notes as possible. Taking notes is a good way to slow down a conversation and allow everyone to think. It also gives you the opportunity to review those notes later to be sure you captured the conversation correctly.
- *Share the results*: Be rigorous in sending out meeting minutes after your client sessions. There's no better way to ensure that everyone heard the same thing than by recording and sharing what transpired and asking for clarification when necessary.[3]

Be aware of your general listening skills, and always remind yourself that hearing your client is more important than hearing yourself speak.[4]

What You Hear in This Pre-Engagement Stage

During the period before the engagement begins, everyone involved very carefully considers the client's concerns and desires. This is the time to listen closely to what your client says. You are likely to learn valuable details that will come in handy once your engagement starts. Even if the client is resistant during pre-engagement phase, listen carefully to the nature of the client's concerns. Record those comments, as they will provide the foundation for the later success of your engagement. Consider the following example:

> *Imagine you will lead a financial accounting software implementation project at a manufacturing corporation. The software chosen is a good fit for the company, but one of the key stakeholders is not in favor of the purchase. Before the contract is finalized, you are invited to a meeting with the executive team to present your implementation plan. That resistant key stakeholder interrupts loudly and often throughout your presentation. He continually brings up his objections and concerns about the software. These have little to do with the actual implementation plan you propose, so most attendees try to ignore what he's saying.*

Analyze a situation such as the one depicted to learn exactly why the resistant client is concerned. Don't try to combat all of the objections or even say very much. Just ask for his patience as you begin the implementation. But listen, very carefully, to his objections and note those well. Consider them a gift. There is probably a great deal of truth in the resistance, and it's that very detail that will help you when you're implementing. You will be able to mirror back those objections with positive solutions when you begin your communication during the engagement.

It's also at this point that many of your clients will probably open up to you. In a way, this is a period of suspended hierarchy. Your engagement has not yet become a part of either the client's operation or its hierarchy. Many within the client organization will likely express their ideas during pre-engagement phase. They may not be intimidated by how something will happen or if it's politically correct to move in a new direction. Savor the candor at this point; listen and learn.

Whatever you hear at this point is likely to be less guarded than it will be later on. During the actual engagement, getting the work at hand done can overshadow the generation of new ideas. Take every opportunity during pre-engagement phase to listen and record what a client says. During the engagement, you can mirror some of these details back to the client in beneficial ways.

Pre-Engagement Audience Analysis

In Chapter 1 we discussed the important audience analysis as the foundation for consultant communication. The simple exercise of evaluating your message from the reader or listener's perspective can yield a more positive reception for your communication. Whether you're delivering routine, good, or bad news, you want your reader to understand and accept it.

We have already reviewed the three general conditions of audience analysis, Situation, Product, and Delivery. Now let's look at how those elements specifically play out in the pre-engagement cycle. Use the following pre-engagement audience analysis as a baseline to create your own.

Exercise 2.1: Pre-engagement

Audience Analysis:

Situation: The pre-engagement period is when your firm is working with the client but hasn't necessarily finalized all contractual matters and the project has not yet begun in earnest.

Value: Your clients likely will be very interested in your communication during pre-engagement because they want to be sure they understand all details before the engagement begins. Whatever you write or present has high impact because you are working to solidify the engagement. They have the time and motivation to devote to this communication. Even your presentations are likely to get full attention. Be precise and concise, however, so you can model future communication during the engagement.

Purpose: This will depend on the specific communication.

Message: This will depend on the specific communication. However, during pre-engagement phase, you may deliver good news to some and bad news to others within the same communication.

Directive: You are most likely presenting your firm's standard materials during pre-engagement phase. You may write or present as a result of a direct request from the client. Regardless, be aware of how much detail you should include or exclude at this point.

Relationship: Your relationship with your client is quite formal and professional at this point, and your communication should mirror that. Some in the audience may not be in favor of the engagement details, so be sensitive to that, especially in your tone and content. Go back and review your notes from prior meetings to understand any objections and reflect those in a positive way in your communication.

Climate and Culture: If you use templates your firm has used in the past, check that they are in line with what the audience is accustomed to. Before you develop a list of addressees or participants, check with the client regarding who to include or exclude.

Deadline: This will depend on the specific communication.

Product: Regardless of what you are delivering in this communication, your output must be extremely professional and lean to the formal.

Wrapper: This will depend on the specific communication; however, you should follow client protocols if possible.

Content: Be very aware of how much your audience members know about the engagement. You are likely presenting introductory materials that need a full explanation and background. While some of the audience may be aware of the information, it's important that you are as detailed and inclusive as possible as you are setting the tone for the entire engagement.

Organization: The audience will value specifics and will probably be patient enough that you can logically present your information from least important to most important points. This is an opportunity to bring your audience around.

Tone: Since you are new to the audience and it to you, be extremely respectful and professional. You should also, however, be relatable and genuine—not too distant. No off-hand remarks or jokes at this point.

Language: Your language must not contain any business or corporate jargon that your audience doesn't understand.

Length: This will depend on the specific communication.

Delivery: You'll need to know how your client typically delivers information and follow that formula. Determine, for example, if virtual meetings are acceptable. Is e-mail the preferred medium? Does the client expect/allow text messaging? Does the client expect many in-person meetings, or should you send information in an e-mail to expedite the communication?

Pre-Engagement Sample Communications

As noted previously, consultants do not always take the communication lead during this stage of the project, but there are some exceptions. In large consulting firms, the account representatives usually send sales and proposal letters, statements of work, and contracts to clients. But in small consulting companies, you may find yourself writing and presenting much of the pre-engagement correspondence. The following examples will provide models for consultants who develop the most common communications during a pre-engagement phase. They include audience analysis exercises and sample documents for the following:

- Sales/Proposal Letter
- SOW
- Project Introduction Presentation
- Meeting Minutes

Sales/Proposal Letter

In business communication, professionals write sales letters to attract new customers to their products and services. Further, they often write these and send them out through mass mailings (e-mail or physical) to a very general audience. However, consultants, especially independent consultants, often write sales/proposal letters to a target audience that has already shown some interest in securing consulting services. This type of sales letter combines several important messages:

- An introduction to the company or consultant(s)
- Some discussion of the business or consultant(s)' achievements and expertise

- A preliminary proposal for required consulting services
- An outline for implementation

Here are some guidelines for writing sales letters:

- Write in a courteous and professional manner, even if you already know the client.
- Be as complete as you can be in who you are and what you or your company can provide. Don't assume your reader knows what you can provide even if you represent a well-known firm.
- Be concrete and direct. Assume there will be multiple readers and that this document will be forwarded.
- Provide general parameters of your offerings but not so detailed that the sale can be rejected just by reading this letter.

Exercise 2.2: Sales/Initial Proposal Letter

Audience Analysis:

Situation: You're writing to a prospective customer who has expressed interest in receiving one month of consulting services to review and redesign a help desk organization. The help desk has not been performing to customer satisfaction and is costing the company too much money. The client will want to know the type of work you are capable of doing but isn't ready to entertain a full proposal.

Value: To focus on the value to the client, highlight some of your achievements. Don't go into too much detail that would suggest that you're limited to one type of engagement.

Purpose: Your purpose is to sell your services within a timeframe that you can achieve optimal results.

Message: Your message must instill confidence in your ability. The client has asked for this sales/proposal letter, so you're clear about your directive. Your relationship with the customer is formal, as you have had no prior dealings. You're unsure of the climate and culture within the organization, so be as professional and neutral as possible in your approach.

Product: You're writing a sales/proposal letter. You want to sell this reader consulting services to improve their help desk organization. Because this is an external client, your wrapper will be a standard, full-block style business letter. The content will include some background on your consulting work and a general description of what you propose to accomplish in the period you will be on-site to consult.

Content: Your content should include a list of activities, a schedule, and expected outcomes. Give the reader enough information to call your firm in for more discussion.

Organization: Organize the letter in a logical way; present yourself, then your general proposal, and then the proposed engagement details. Your tone must be professional and polished as you want to make a great impression. Be sure to write in general language about the topic, as this audience may not be familiar with some of the terms you may use during the engagement.

Length: This is not a full proposal but an initial sales/proposal, so keep the letter to no more than one-and-a-half pages so the reader can review the material quickly and respond.

Delivery: Since the prospective client e-mailed you, your delivery will also be via e-mail. However, don't reply only via the more casual e-mail method. Since you are a professional, send as a business letter on letterhead and attach a pdf version of the letter document to an e-mail.

Sales/Initial Proposal Letter Example

Diversified Consulting Services, Inc.
123 S. Main Street
Chester, VT 03257

December 15, 2016

Ms. Janet Mercurion
Executive Director for User Services
Comcon Utilities
140 Bridgetown Street
New Haven, CT 02395

Dear Ms. Mercurion:

Thank you for your recent inquiry about Diversified   Why you're
Consulting Services, Inc. I am writing to provide you with   writing
information about our consulting services and to present
you with some ways we might help you strengthen your
Help Desk organization.

As a consulting firm dedicated to providing personalized   Who you
services for our clients, we employ defined methodolo-   are
gies that achieve optimum results. However, what makes
us stand apart is that we specialize in providing individualized consulting services matched to your firm's specific
needs.

We are very interested in providing consultation and   What you
advising for members of your team who want to revi-   can do
talize your Help Desk services. Our work with over 20
technology companies on similar projects has helped us
establish a proven track record in helping firms improve
customer service.

So that you can move quickly to make improvements,   The plan
we propose the following sequence of activities that can
move us ahead:

- In the next week, our senior consultant can
  meet with your Help Desk managers to determine the scope of the project.
- By January 15, we will reply with a detailed
  statement of work to include project scope,
  deliverables, roles and responsibilities, and
  costs.
- By February 1, we can begin interviews with
  your staff and managers.
- By March 1, we will present our findings,
  recommendations, and implementation plan.

Thank you very much for your interest in our services. We appreciate the opportunity to work with you. I will call your assistant, Jenny, later this week to arrange a time for us to discuss this individualized process for optimizing your Help Desk function.

Congenial farewell and specific next steps

Sincerely,

James D. Cowens

James D. Cowens
President

Statement of Work

An SOW defines what a vendor will deliver as part of a particular project or engagement. As a consultant, you may be asked to write an SOW as part of a proposal, contract, or project plan. The SOW is a very particular scope document that details the major deliverables, tasks, governance structure, schedule, costs, and resources required for an engagement. It's important to get it right because it identifies all the major components of what's ahead. As Mary Pratt wrote in *Computerworld*, "If the statement of work is too vague, too broad, or too generic, it can leave room for various interpretations, which can lead to trouble down the road. That's true for an internal project, and it's doubly true when there are vendors involved."[5] This doesn't mean that every detail needs to be spelled out, especially for a simple or small project, but it does mean that you need enough information to be sure you and your client have the same expectations for the work ahead.

Follow these tips when writing an SOW:

- Reference any previous sales letter or notes to ensure you include all information your client expects.
- Include your scope, activities, roles and responsibilities, and schedule, at the least.
- Write in a clear, concise manner with no jargon. This document will be shared with many so it needs to translate for all readers.

- Use headings, bulleted lists, and boldface to illustrate clear organization.

Exercise 2.3: Statement of Work

Audience Analysis:

Situation: Your small business consulting company has an excellent opportunity to perform a medium-size business process redesign on a major company's help desk operation. Your client is keenly interested in moving ahead quickly, so be sure that your communication emphasizes this with details, not rhetoric. That will be the value to the client.

Purpose: Your purpose in writing this piece is to describe deliverables, responsibilities and schedule so your message will be good news to those reading it. It will be scrutinized, so you need to get it right. The customer has requested this information, so your directive is clear. Your relationship with the client is formal at this point, and your prose needs to reflect that. They are a large company, so the climate and culture is very business oriented and professional. Your document needs to mirror that orientation. Your deadline is ASAP, as they want to begin work immediately, so get this out today.

Product: Your information will be entered in a formal Statement of Work (SOW) template that is acceptable in a business environment. That SOW wrapper will follow standard protocols, and you need to check if your client has a standard they would like to use. Also add a brief cover letter as part of the delivery.

Content: The content will include the required project scope, deliverables, activities, and a schedule, and it is organized in a template form including these elements. Multiple audiences will read this piece, from the executive who receives it, to the managers who will be most affected by the change. Your tone and language must be specific enough to allow for agreement but general enough that you don't narrow down your options too much.

Length: The template will determine the length.

Delivery: Deliver the document via e-mail but as an attachment. Also provide the SOW in paper form, for signature and return.

Statement of Work Example

Statement of Work

for

Comcon Utilities Help Desk Redesign Project
Provided by Diversified Consulting Services, Inc.

Project Introduction

Over the past 18 months, Comcon Utilities doubled its corporate accounts and added approximately 200 new customers to its client base. Over the past six months, there has been a sharp rise in customer service problems for those calling the help desk. Complaints include long wait times on hold and inability to solve problems on the first try. Help Desk employee morale is down, and the staff complains about high stress levels, lack of metrics, little direction, and inability to resolve problems effectively.

Mutual understanding of project background

Comcon has a goal to improve its help desk customer service over the next six months. It has established a Help Desk Redesign Project and has engaged Diversified Consulting Services, Inc. to lead it.

Scope

The Help Desk Redesign Project is responsible for creating a design and implementation plan to improve Help Desk customer service over the next six months. Diversified Consulting Services, Inc. will facilitate the planning by working with Comcon's internal project team to review and redesign, where necessary, all processes, organization, and technology related to Help Desk operations. Comcon expects project design

General parameters of project

outcomes will include improved customer service, better metrics for ongoing operations, and improved staff training and support. The Help Desk Redesign Project is responsible for creating a plan for improvement that can be implemented within six months, but it should also include any longer term opportunities that Comcon should address in regard to Help Desk operations.

Activities and Responsibilities

The Help Desk Redesign Project team will be made up of internal Comcon staff and Diversified Consulting Services, Inc. personnel. The project team will be co-led by an internal Comcon manager and a principal consultant from Diversified Consulting Services, Inc.

Who will do what

The following activities will be conducted over the project lifecycle:

Project Introduction:

- Diversified Consulting Services, Inc. will create and present a project plan including team responsibilities, schedule, analysis, deliverables, and implementation plan for Comcon's review and sign off.

Analysis and Design:

- Diversified Consulting Services, Inc. will lead the Help Desk Redesign Project Team to analyze all Help Desk processes, activities, metrics, and operations.
- Diversified Consulting Services, Inc. will lead the Help Desk Redesign Project Team to interview all Help Desk staff to identify organizational issues.

- Diversified Consulting Services, Inc. will facilitate the Help Desk Redesign Project to review the current efficacy of Help Desk technologies. The project team will also evaluate new technologies for possible adoption.

Project Planning:

- The Help Desk Redesign Project Team will develop and deliver a plan for new processes, organization, and technology that improve Help Desk customer service.
- The Help Desk Redesign Project Team will design and provide a high-level implementation plan that can be enacted over the next six months.

Project Wrap Up:

- Diversified Consulting Services, Inc. will provide Comcon with all project data files, documentation, and plans.
- The Help Desk Redesign Project Team will present its findings to the Comcon Executive Team for final review and approval.

Schedule

- January 10, 2017: Project kickoff meeting
- February 1, 2017: Process reviews completed
- February 10, 2017: Staff interviews completed, metrics analyzed
- February 15, 2017: Technology review completed
- March 1, 2017:   Help Desk Redesign Project Plan presented for consideration and approval

What will happen when

Additional Requirements

All employees of Diversified Consulting Services, Inc. must sign a Comcon Nondisclosure agreement.

Any additional details

Statement of Work Acceptance

_____

Date:_____

Comcon Utilities Approver

SOW approvals

_____

Date:_____

Diversified Consulting Services, Inc. Approver[6]

Project Introduction Presentation

One of the first presentations you will make is to formally introduce the engagement to your clients. If you're a consultant in a large firm, you probably already have access to a temple for a project/engagement introduction presentation. It's likely standard. If you're an independent consultant, you will need to create your own. Regardless of the circumstances, you should know how to introduce new materials to your clients.

By the time you put together an introductory presentation, you already have much of the detail you will include. The contract may not be officially signed yet, but you have worked out the details with your client participants. They are anxious to inform their staff of what's about to happen. Your company will have already sent the client a variety of correspondence probably including a preliminary sales proposal, a sample contract or SOW, a pricing proposal, product and services briefs, and corporate profiles. Depending on the timing of this presentation, you must carefully consider what you will include in it. If your contract isn't signed, you may not yet be able to share all specifics about the project. However, the prior correspondence with the client will provide you with many details that you can easily incorporate into your introductory presentation. Your audience analysis will help you as you develop this communication and here are some tips to guide you:

- Get to the point quickly. This information may be more important to you than to your audience so don't overestimate it.
- Mirror the information found in the contractual materials. Don't bring new elements in that have not been agreed upon.
- Add only a few lines of information on each slide. Save the details for your oral description.
- Add only as many slides as the meeting time allows. Be sure to leave enough time for discussion.

Exercise 2.4: Project Introduction Presentation

Audience Analysis:

Situation: The small business consulting firm you work for has been hired to conduct an engagement with a major telecommunications company. The contract has not yet been finalized, but the client has asked for a project kickoff meeting to expedite the project. Your company will provide consulting services to facilitate a business process redesign of the customer's help desk operation. This situation now calls for you to present a high level project plan. You will lead the project as senior consultant/project manager.

Value: The client will value any details that will garner the management and staff support.

Message: The client wants to move quickly on this project, so your message must be clear and upbeat. Because the contract is not finalized, there are some details you might not be able to include (such as who will be assigned internally to the project team). However, you must communicate a firm sense of direction so that will include a specific timeline for project completion. The help desk personnel will make up most of the audience.

Climate: The client has been under pressure with a significant increase in customer base and increased customer complaints over the past several months. So, the climate is currently stressed, and the culture is one of concerned and demoralized staff. Your presentation is tomorrow, so you need to complete this by today's 1 p.m. deadline and pass it along to your boss for review and approval.

Product: The product is a presentation at tomorrow's kickoff meeting.

Wrapper: The wrapper should be a PowerPoint presentation with your company's standard logo.

Content: Include a general description of the goals of the project, making sure you are in sync with what the key client has told her managers and staff. Organize your materials from a logical flow, first introducing your company, then the project, and then the project specifics. Most of the audience is unaware of the details already agreed upon, so carefully avoid any volatile details. The tone and language should leave room for some discussion, but firmly state what you are doing as that has already been decided. This will be the trickiest part of creating the presentation. The presentation is scheduled for one hour, so keep it brief to allow for discussion.

Length: Length should be under 10 slides (3 minutes each). This will allow for a maximum of 30 minutes of presentation and 30 minutes of discussion. Deliver the PowerPoint via e-mail to the client to allow for his feedback. Make any last minute changes just before the meeting.

Project Introduction Presentation Example

[Design using company template and color palette.]
Comcon Utilities
Help Desk Redesign Project

Diversified Consulting Services, Inc. (DCS)
Abigail Potter, Senior Consultant
January 10, 2017

Diversified Consulting Services, Inc.
(DCS)

- James D. Cowens, President and CEO
- Abigail Potter, Senior Consultant and Project Leader
- Andrew Solo, Data Analytics Specialist
- Peter Jordan, Help Desk Redesign Expert

Project Goals

- Redesign Help Desk operations to improve customer service within six months
- Develop an implementation plan to achieve the redesign

Project Description

- The Help Desk Redesign Project is responsible for creating a design and implementation plan to improve Help Desk customer service over the next six months.
- Diversified Consulting Services, Inc. will facilitate the planning with Comcon Utilities' internal project team
- The project team will review and redesign relevant processes, organization, and technology

Expected outcomes

A plan for:
- Improved customer service
- Enhanced staff training and support
- Better metrics for ongoing operations
- World class Help Desk technologies

Team Resources

People
- Comcon will form a team of managers and subject matter experts to work with DCS on this project

Location
- All work will be conducted at the Comcon Boston office

Support and outside services
- DCS will provide all support technologies and services to develop the plan

Schedule

- January 10, 2017:   Project Kickoff meeting
- February 1, 2017:   Process Reviews completed
- February 10, 2017: Staff interviews completed, metrics analyzed
- February 15, 2017: Technology review completed
- March 1, 2017:   Help Desk Redesign Project Plan presented

Questions?

Contacts:

Jim Cowens
james.cowens@dcs.xxx

Abby Potter
abigail.potter@dcs.xxx

Meeting Minutes

Whether meetings are held in person or virtually, we all seem to be in a constant cycle of attending meetings. We meet before engagements, during engagements, and after engagements. Often we even meet to plan more meetings. While we won't spend time here scrutinizing what makes up a good or bad meeting, we will discuss why it is important to keep track of what goes on in any meeting, especially in the consultant/ client relationship. You will produce minutes throughout all phases of an engagement, but it's good to get in the habit of doing just that as soon as you begin to meet with your client during pre-engagement phase.

Meeting minutes provide a useful way to document the major topics, assignments, motions, and decisions made in meetings. A consultant is wise to keep track of all of these matters, as the meeting minutes may be the only record of what transpires in the sessions. In a swiftly moving project it becomes difficult to stop and record meeting activity. Whether you record formally or informally, on paper or with technology, you should do it. Here, we will consider the most formal version of published meeting minutes. However, remember that even just producing notes from your meetings and sending them to all parties in attendance will help you down the road. There's nothing worse than arriving at a disagreement between consultant and client without any backup documentation to support your claims. Follow this advice when writing meeting minutes:

- Follow your client's meeting minutes format if there is one. If not, standardize your own.
- Write the minutes as a record of what is discussed. Do not elaborate on any of the points made.
- Use the simple past tense when referring to what was said.
- Include the names of attendees, those absent, and guests. Be sure to add the company or department each attendee represents.
- Mention the date of the next meeting.
- Include your name if you prepared the minutes.[7]

Exercise 2.5: Meeting Minutes

Audience Analysis:

Situation: The Comcon Utilities Help Desk Redesign Project has been operating since January 10; that's the current situation. The redesign project team has met informally every two days since the work began, but it meets more formally on particular milestone days. Today's meeting is such a day.

Value: Document this meeting to ensure all parties are in sync as you approach the end of the project. Also, your senior executive clients will find value in receiving these formal minutes so they know that all parties are aware of the project status. Your purpose in writing these minutes is to document your status, especially since you are behind on some of your milestone deliverables. The project team and all executives need to know that you are running behind.

Message: Your message, via the minutes, will be clear and direct with no editorial comments or explanations, simply facts. Your relationship with the client has become less formal since you are working closely together, but be more formal in these official minutes than you are in everyday checklist e-mails. Your deadline to distribute these minutes is no later than 24 hours after the meeting.

Product: The product is a document that follows a standard business meeting minutes wrapper.

Content: The content should include standard minutes information including date, time, leader, location, attendees and absences, guests, time started, reports by topic, next meeting topics, and next meeting time and place. Your tone should be professional. Write using simple, clear language with no elaboration, simply stating facts. Write in the past tense.

Delivery: Deliver the minutes as an attachment to an e-mail and file it with project documents.

Meeting Minutes Example

COMCON UTILITIES HELP DESK REDESIGN PROJECT	Project Description
PROJECT TEAM MEETING MINUTES	Minutes Title
February 10, 2017	Date and
Comcon Utilities Executive Offices Bridgetown Street, Boston, MA	Location

Attendees:

Representing Diversified Consulting Services, Inc—Abigail Potter, Andrew Solo, Peter Jordan (not in attendance: James Cowens)	Attendees and Absentees
Representing Comcon Utilities—John Wilkins, Madison Lee, Rodrigo Babbitt (not in attendance: Jim Bates, John McGowan, and Willow Windemere)	Meeting Facilitator

Meeting Moderator: Abigail Potter, Senior Consultant, Diversified Consulting Services, Inc. (DCS)

The meeting began at 8:35 a.m.

The minutes from the January 31 meeting were approved.

Business Process Redesign Update: Peter Jordan reported that 80% of the business process redesign (BPR) has been completed. His group will send a report out tomorrow. Preliminary results indicate that the most urgent design issue resolves around developing new methods of escalating calls. Andrew Solo stated that the data in the customer services logs are inconsistent and may prove difficult to analyze. He promised to update the team on his progress by e-mail by EOD, February 11. The new estimate for a complete BPR is February 15.	Updates by Project Topic

Organization Redesign Update: Abigail Potter and Rodrigo Babbitt reported that all staff members have been interviewed. Mr. Babbitt is currently summarizing the results and reported he will be ready to present new organizational models on February 15.

Technology Redesign Update: Peter Jordan, Andrew Solo, and Adriana Staten (Comcon) have completed their help desk technology solutions review. They are prepared to make recommendations to the project team on February 15.

Overall Redesign Update: Abigail Potter reported that the project is running five days behind schedule, but she estimated being able to complete the redesign plan by the due date of March 1.

Next meeting: February 15, 2017

The meeting ended at 9:30 a.m.

Prepared by: Rodrigo Babbitt

Next meeting date
Time adjournment
Preparer

Chapter Conclusion

The pre-engagement phase of a consulting project is an exciting yet delicate time. It's a time filled with client aspirations, hopes, fears, and often skepticism. You arrive at pre-engagement phase filled with energy for your new engagement, but you meet as strangers. Your communication must be top notch, as what you write and present in these early days can make a lasting impression.

During this period, it is imperative to listen carefully; what you hear now will resonate throughout the engagement. Preparing audience analyses before you communicate is critical to your success. Using samples and good business communication standards as guides can help you master the process, put your best foot forward, and make your clients comfortable as you begin to work with one another.

CHAPTER 3

Engagement Communication

We've explored the communications that consultants encounter as they approach an engagement. In this chapter, we will turn our attention to the actual engagement, that period extending from when the contract is signed through the project completion. In our discussion, we will:

- review types of communication during this phase,
- detail the environment from both a consultant and a client's perspective,
- discuss key communication considerations during this phase,
- highlight advice for new consultants,
- illustrate best approaches to essential communications during this phase, and
- provide tips for writing and presenting engagement communications.

The Engagement Phase

The engagement phase is the period when the action begins for a consultant. You not only contribute to communications during the engagement but also often own them. As part of the consultant role you, of course, not only communicate quite a bit yourself but also coordinate much of the communication within the project. A multitude of tasks and people are swirling around during an engagement, and managing the communication output can be a significant challenge. As a consultant, you will need to keep focused on all materials created since these make up the project's official documentation.

Engagements can run from one day to many years. During this period, much of the work is organized around agree-upon milestones, deliverables, and outputs. Correspondences, reports, presentations, and specifications abound. From the time the engagement begins until it ends, all communications combine to form the essence of the project. In a technology-related project, the final deliverable may be a new computer system, but in a management consulting project, a written plan may be the output that completes the contract. To produce these deliverables, multiple writers, presenters, and audiences begin to blend and transform. Your working team now includes members from your firm as well as from your client's organization. Team members are working across organization and hierarchies. An entirely new management structure suddenly emerges, and the rules change.

With this new organizational mix comes differing communication styles, formats, and protocols, all of which must be coordinated around a new entity—the project team. The consultant must be ready to take on the challenges of managing and producing top quality materials in a fast-paced, diverse environment.

The Engagement Communication

As we discussed in Chapter 1, many large firms have standard communication templates that they use to enable the speedy creation of materials. If you are part of a smaller firm or are an independent consultant, it's likely you will create these materials yourself, just as you did during pre-engagement phase. All consultants must recognize, however, that a template for organizing and adding information is only a part of the engagement communication story. Because a client is now paying for services, how something is written or presented in terms of organization, tone, style, content, and delivery is as important as the template that envelops it.

The abundant communications during engagement run from informal to formal. A variety of routine communications, such as e-mails and texts, is continually developed. However, you also prepare many formal pieces of correspondence, reports, and presentations. Business correspondence standards become an important element of the engagement because everything written is part of the record. Since engagements can run for a long period, having these standards in place as accessible artifacts can also determine the success of a project. A successful consultant doesn't take the creation or management of an engagement's communication for granted.

Let's now turn our attention to some of the types of communications commonly written and presented during an engagement.

Early Engagement Communication

As an engagement begins, consultants either prepare or contribute to the preparation of several start-up communications. These early communications include the following types.

Team Introductions: Most engagements begin with the consulting firm introducing itself to the client. Since a new entity is being formed, the introduction typically presents all members of the consulting team and those of the client. This can be accomplished in presentation style, or all team members can introduce themselves in a meeting, but it works well if the audience learns a little about each team member's background, expertise, and project role.

Project Plans: The project manager of the engagement usually creates and manages the project plans that reflect the project schedule, tasks, outcomes, and deliverables. Often, the original Statement of Work (SOW) or contract is used as the foundation for the initial project plan. The project plan also typically includes a risk analysis of the project and project details including team membership information, interdependencies details, and milestone definitions.

Communication Plans: Along with the overall project plan, there is typically a separate but connected communication plan. Communication plans capture the timing, source (deliverer), audience, delivery mechanism, and frequency of anticipated communications.

Again, the project manager creates and manages this artifact, though consultants and various other team members contribute to it on an ongoing basis. Many of the engagement communications we discuss in this chapter would be tracked within this communication plan.

Team Operating Procedures: As part of your team introduction, you will likely present the overall operating procedures for the project. This will include how engagement work will be managed, how team members will interact with one another, how decisions will be made, and how issues will be dealt with and resolved. While these procedures might be presented in a meeting, they will likely be documented in writing and held by the project manager.

Project Vision Statements: One of the first pieces of communication to emerge during an engagement is a vision statement for the project. This is usually a brief statement that identifies the overall goal for the team and for the project. It defines what is possible and is used to encourage the team to forge ahead to achieve desired results.[1]

Routine Ongoing Communication

At the heart of the engagement is a series of ongoing communications that supports the work of the project. These communications fuel the work of the engagement team and document its progress.

Correspondence—e-mails, letters, and texts: Just as in any organization, the engagement team routinely communicates via e-mail on a daily if not hourly basis. Some of the e-mails are rather informal and internal to the team. Some may have a more formal letter from the consulting firm to the client as an attachment. There is also a good chance that the group will use text messages as part of its normal operations. Informal or formal, these communications still need attention and scrutiny. In fact, sometimes they need more oversight since they don't pass through the typical team management channels.

Team meetings, presentations, and minutes: These routine sessions and communications are constant during an engagement. Meetings, which can be conducted in person or virtually, are organized by the project or team leaders and are held on a regular schedule, such as daily or weekly. The output from these meetings is also typically routinized, so the actual documentation doesn't interfere with the efficacy of the work carried out in the sessions.

Instructions: Often consultants need to guide their teams or clients and document procedures. They write clear and concise instructions to set direction, standardize activities, and move tasks along.

Reports—trip, progress, and periodic: Part of a consulting engagement usually involves the research and reporting of information. This process results in written or orally presented reports. Trip reports, for instance, record the activities and outcomes of a particular excursion. Engagement progress and other periodic reports detail the status of activities, schedules, and budgets.[2]

Milestone Communications

Milestones define a project within the overall plan. Depending on the length of the engagement, there may be regularly scheduled milestones or they may be attached to particular outcomes or deliverables. In a small engagement, the only significant milestone might be concluding the project and producing a report. In all cases, milestone communications tend to be formal and directed toward project sponsors and client executives.

Executive Meetings, Presentations, and Minutes

Not a milestone goes by without a project team meeting and reporting to client executives, sponsors, and process owners. The project team, usually with previous collaboration of the executive sponsor, carefully constructs these meeting agendas, presentations, and minutes. The output is formal and an important part of the official project documentation.

Investigative Reports

Often consultants deliver data reports at engagement milestones. Investigative reports consist of an examination of collected data, analysis of those data, conclusions, and, depending on the situation, recommendations. Whether a sponsor or executive specifically requests a study or you as the consultant decide to investigate a matter, the report follows a particular standard organization.[3]

Project Formal Reports

Regardless of the length or complexity of an engagement, it will typically wrap up with a formal report, both in oral presentation form and in writing. Depending on the engagement, the report will include a variety of content areas. Most formal reports, however, include the following: title page, table of contents, abstract, executive summary, introduction, presentation of findings, conclusions, and recommendations.[4]

Examples and tips for writing various types of engagement communications are located at the end of this chapter.

The Engagement Environment

Consultants and clients alike face an engagement knowing that they will have their work cut out for them. Some consulting engagements begin gently and others with a bang. Some engagements are brief and simple, and others are extended and complex. Regardless, there is work involved and project sponsors expect outcomes. From the outset, this is a busy time. The engagement is scheduled for a set period; therefore, from the first working day, all parties are under pressure to keep to the established timeline.

When the engagement begins, the players are typically new to one another. Even if you have consulted for a particular client before, the circumstances are new. During engagement start-up, new working relationships develop. In most large engagements, new cross-functional and cross-company teams are formed. Consultants, project managers, analysts, subject matter experts, process owners, and technologists are suddenly thrown together to work as a new highly functioning unit. New leadership emerges and new processes and operations form. Even a consultant who has been working in a large firm for a while faces new team leadership and membership. For the client, there is usually radical change. Individuals may find themselves on a new team working with members of other internal and external entities.

It's as if everyone is an athlete playing for his team, and suddenly players are sent to an All-Star Game to play and win on a new team made up of opponents. It's unsettling and confusing. But that's where good consultants step in to ease the transition and move the contributors ahead.

As the engagement progresses, contributors and consultants form a new entity, no matter how brief, and work is accomplished. The communications of that new entity shift, too. The work of the engagement takes priority, and communication is an underpinning of that work. Audiences become more accustomed to one another, and all the players become more comfortable to present, meet, and write with one another. It's at this very moment during the engagement when everyone is more used to one another that consultants must keep professionalism at the forefront of communications. Audience analysis becomes more critical than ever during this time of shifting roles.

Let's now focus on the specifics regarding consultants and clients within the engagement period to establish the foundation for strong audience analysis.

What the Consultant Brings to the Environment

As the consultant, you are the expert. You may be an expert on the subject matter of the engagement, and you are surely the expert on how to work within the engagement. So, whether you are the engagement manager, team leader, or a supporting consultant, you are viewed as having great expertise. You are vital to the success of any engagement. You help clear the path to productivity and move the work along. Remember this when you communicate, because what you say carries weight.

It's important to any firm that an engagement succeeds, and consultants carry that burden. As a lead consultant, you may have ultimate responsibility for many of the deliverables within an engagement. You find yourself with many moving parts and many people, processes, and data to oversee. It's your responsibility to clear a path to be productive, so how quickly a team can form and begin to work effectively often lies with you. You also need to satisfy various interest groups including your boss, the client, and the teams you lead or work with. The pressures are very real, but the rewards can be, too.

Over your time as a consultant, you will weave your way through an engagement and achieve positive results. To do this, though, it's important that you instill confidence in your expertise and the work you represent. An important way you will do is this through effective communications. In everything and in every way you communicate, you must remain open, politically neutral, and flexible. This is easier said than done when pressures mount from disagreements on the team, data overload, scheduling challenges, and more. You have a job to do and deadlines to meet, but don't let that overshadow listening to your client and your team members. Having awareness about how and when to communicate improves your chances of success.

How the Client Comes to the Environment

It's worth a close look at what your client brings to the actual engagement phase and how that influences your communication. As we discussed in Chapter 2, any disruption is difficult for a client. So, especially in the early stages of the engagement, many of the pre-engagement emotions and thoughts remain. Some on the client team may take some time to move from trepidation toward complete embracing of the engagement. Just because a contract has been signed does not mean that all the skepticism, avoidance, fear of change, and uncertainty disappear.

The sheer effort of the engagement may make it appear daunting. Your client or members of the engagement team may never have worked on a project of this magnitude or on any project with clear deliverables and milestones. The time your client team spends on the engagement may be in addition to their regular work. Members of the team may be used to leaving promptly at 5 p.m. to now learn that the work isn't done until the milestone is accomplished, regardless of the time on the clock. From the client's perspective, mastering new consulting language, processes, documentation, and protocols might seem overwhelming. This puts the onus on the consultant to carefully yet confidently communicate with clients to prepare them for the engagement and to not appear frustrated with cultural work differences.

Beyond the added work, engagements also demand openness, and this can often present an additional challenge. As the consultant, you'll need information before drawing conclusions and making recommendations, and you'll need to count on clients to provide you with accurate and honest details about how and why things work in particular ways. No one is immune to worries about telling an outside consultant how exactly they spend their time or why they made a particular policy decision. It takes time to trust a consultant, so you must use your discretion to gauge that factor.

One of the biggest shifts from pre-engagement to engagement comes in the form of what emerges to be "The Real Story." During pre-engagement phase, your firm proposes a project or program based on how it understands the current situation. Sometimes, for example, a company is taking too long to ship its products and asks for a plan to implement new fulfillment management processes and systems. Usually, after some general discussions and analysis, your firm and the client determine what the engagement should look like. And typically that analysis is logical and valid. However, once the engagement begins, consultants often hear "The Real Story." That story might emerge from client representatives who were not able to contribute during the proposal stage. It also might come from others who see matters differently and want to set you, the consultant, straight. This situation may result when process owners complain that management doesn't understand what they do. Or you may hear that the technology, not organizational factors, is the problem for the firm. No matter how it emerges, "The Real Story" should be regarded as an attempt to resist the efforts of the engagement as agreed upon by its sponsors. In these circumstances, your communication with the storytellers and with your sponsors will be challenging and sensitive. You're caught in the middle, and the need for honest and discreet communication is paramount.

On the positive side of the engagement phase, many clients and members of your own staff develop new skills during a project. There is much opportunity for people to excel and develop, and many will rise to become new leaders. They may be keen to take on new work, and they will drive hard to complete tasks on time. Watch for these eager contributors. If you can effectively channel their enthusiasm into good work and great communication, they will do much to help you and your project succeed.

Communication Considerations During an Engagement

With the environmental factors we just reviewed as a backdrop, let's consider some key elements that will support your communications during an engagement:

- **Practice professionalism.** Everything you write or present is a reflection of your professional persona. Be sure your messages are based on fact and that you are considerate of your audience. Excellent communication will help you maintain your integrity, which is paramount to your success.

- **Be precise and to the point**. Don't say more than you
  need to. Drive to the specifics and honor everyone's time
  constraints.[5]
- **Learn how to deliver good news and bad news**. There's a
  method that works best in each circumstance. Become familiar with these.
- **Strive for clarity**. Make sure everyone understands what you
  mean. Engagements are not the time for confusion.
- **Make sure your engagement-critical communications are
  perfect**. Edit them well and ask others to help you do that,
  too.
- **Listen closely to your clients and colleagues**. Say less than
  you might want to say, and carefully regard what others are
  expressing.
- **Employ the "no surprises" rule**. Don't bring up sensitive
  matters in meetings without first vetting those in advance.
- **Use appropriate medium to communicate your message**.
  Use e-mails, texts, letters, conference calls, virtual meetings,
  and one-on-one meetings as they best relate to the message
  and the audience, not only to your liking.
- **Present materials in a logical way to best illustrate your
  points**. Organize your written and oral communication in
  a way that best reflects the needs of your audience, not just
  what first comes to mind.

Special Communication Advice for New Consultants Assigned to an Engagement

If you're new to consulting, you may learn much of what we discuss here
on the job, actually during an engagement. It's very common for a new
consultant to determine the logistics of an engagement but not necessarily how to communicate during this period. However, whether you work
for a large firm, for a small consulting company, or as an independent
consultant, these communication tips will help you communicate during
an engagement.

- **Analyze your audience before communicating with it**. Every situation is different in business, and every audience has different needs. You are no longer writing to one person as you might have in the past, so you need to calculate what you say and how you say it for a particular situation.
- **When you write or present, tell the audience members what's in it for them**. Don't assume they know what you know, and don't make them work to understand why you're communicating. Respect their time.
- **Practice good business writing and presenting techniques**. Don't make it up as you go along, and don't assume you should communicate as you did in college. Professional writing and presenting are more direct, and you need to adjust your communication accordingly. Pick up a good handbook such as *The Business Writer's Handbook*, by Alred, Brusaw, and Oliu for tips on business writing and presenting.[6]
- **Practice your presentations in advance**. Be sure you can clearly state your message and that you've said the words in advance and out loud. Make sure you leave room for discussion on major points.
- **Write in the active rather than the passive voice as much as possible**. You'll have a better chance of getting your points across without confusing who should do what.
- **Separate your professional communication from your personal communication**. Use your company e-mail address only for your work. Personal matters, even if you're interacting with a client on a personal issue, need to stay separate.
- **Be aware of client use of communication medium and technology**. Some clients will never want you to text them. Others might. Your manager will steer you in the right direction; but if you're an independent consultant, you need to evaluate what to do and when. Don't assume that the way you communicate is the way everyone does.
- **Be discreet with engagement information and stay away from team and project politics, especially with clients**. As an

engagement unfolds, all parties will want to talk about the work they are doing. Stay neutral and keep away from engagement gossip, especially in writing. Define a code of conduct for yourself if your company doesn't have one and live by it.

- **Listen well**. Take this opportunity to learn from your team members and clients. Resist the urge to prove you know more about the topic than anyone else.
- **Be culturally aware**. Companies, like countries, have unique cultures. Respect these and don't impose your values on others during the engagement. Be very aware of how your communications reflect your professionalism and that of your firm.

Engagement Audience Analysis

The shift to an active engagement affects your view of the audience and potentially creates some communication challenges. You enter the engagement period as a stranger, and you hope to leave as a friend. In reality, you are neither. Problems develop when a consultant tries to fit in and become an insider. On the one hand, you may work on a project for two years. It's natural that you will get to know your client colleagues well, and that's a positive for ongoing communication and positive interaction. On the other hand, you still represent an outside entity, so your professional demeanor cannot slip.

As the project progresses and you work closely with your client, multiple audiences need even closer examination. You will often find yourself managing competing interests, and you may need to communicate unpopular views, as illustrated in the case that follows.

Minicase 3.1: Fingering the Boss

The owner of a small insurance company has hired you to help increase its marketing reach to a national audience. The company recently invested significant resources into a new website. As you interview key staff and evaluate the website, you learn that several policies and procedures now in place have been the reason for the site's poor performance. You also learn that the owner who hired you made those policy and process decisions.

The day arrives, and you must present your findings to the company, managers, and staff alike. The boss, himself, will be at the meeting so tensions are high. Of course, you talk to the owner and let him know before sharing this information with the staff. If you're lucky, the owner encourages transparency and wants to share the information with all audiences.

1. What do you do if the owner doesn't want the sensitive information shared with the staff?
2. How do you keep your integrity and still satisfy your key sponsor?

Negotiating ways to deliver bad news without damaging your client relationship is complex. During the engagement, you will spend a significant amount of energy strategizing around situations like these. How do you share information? When do you share information? With whom do you share information? These questions will drive your audience analysis every time you write or present. As we have discussed, consultants and all writers and presenters should spend the time analyzing their audiences, especially when offering engagement-critical communications. This analysis is of particular importance during the engagement because of the variety of audiences and communications involved.

Just as we did in considering the pre-engagement phase, let's turn our attention to the three general conditions of audience analysis, Situation, Product, and Delivery. You can use the following comprehensive audience analysis as a baseline to create your own during the engagement period.

Exercise 3.1: Engagement

Audience Analysis:

Situation: The engagement period starts when the contract has been finalized and the work begins. You begin interacting directly with the client. The phase ends when all deliverables have been completed.

Value: There are many audiences within an engagement. While each is interested in your messages, you need to craft targeted communication for different groups. At various times, you will write and present to client executives, your managers, project sponsors, process owners, subject matter experts, and team members. Early in the engagement, your audiences will be very interested in your communication because they want to be sure they understand all details of the project and expectations. Later on that interest might waver, so you'll need to continue to assess the audience's need for information. Whatever you write or present is engagement-critical because you are working to meet deadlines. Early on your client will make the time and be motivated to give attention to your communication and presentations. As the engagement progresses, however, you will compete with other client interests. You will need to be acutely aware of the value your communication has to the audience.

Purpose: This will depend on the specific communication.

Message: This will depend on the specific communication. Many engagement communications are simple information transfer pieces. However, at milestones you will create engagement-critical communications.

Directive: You will most likely be presenting your firm's standard materials during an engagement. These will have been agreed upon as part of the project or communications plan. Occasionally, however, you will be asked to prepare materials *ad hoc*, especially if problems arise.

Relationship: Your relationship with the client is quite formal and professional at the beginning of the engagement, and your communication should mirror that. Over time, the project team members especially will become more familiar with one another. It will be important to assess if your communication is more routine, thus less formal, or more engagement-critical, thus more formal. This difference will depend not only on the message itself but also on the reason for the message. If the communication is regarded as a permanent part of the engagement, it must be formal. If it is a simple e-mail transaction, it can be less formal. In either case, even if your relationship with the client becomes more familiar, all communication must be professional.

Climate and Culture: If you use templates your firm has used in the past, check that they are in line with audience expectations. As you bring new templates into the engagement, check with the client to be sure they are acceptable artifacts for this environment. Before developing a list of addressees or participants, check with the client as to who to include or exclude.

Deadline: This will depend on the particular communication.

Product: This will depend on the reason for the specific communication. In this engagement phase, however, there will be a variety of outputs produced. These often include correspondence, reports, and instructions, to name a few.

Wrapper: This will depend on the specific communication; however, follow your firm and client protocols.

Content: Be very aware of how much your audience members know about the engagement. You likely will present introductory materials that need a full explanation with more background. You may also give new information that might take effort for the audience to digest. Balancing detail with a particular audience, and sometimes a mixed consulting/client audience, will guide what to include and exclude. Be ready to present backup detail in case it's required. Some audiences want you to get to the point, but others may ask for more detail. If you're presenting, have this backup information ready.

Organization: The audience will value specifics and is probably patient enough that you can logically present information from least important to most important points. This is an opportunity to bring your audience around. When presenting conclusions and recommendations, however, get to the point as quickly as possible, especially for executive audiences.

Tone: Be extremely respectful and professional, even when engagement personnel have become familiar with one another.

Language: Language must be understandable to the client audience and not contain any consulting or corporate jargon that the audience doesn't understand.

Length: This will depend on the specific communication.

Delivery: You'll need to know how both your firm and the client typically deliver information and follow those protocols. If you are an independent consultant, prepare materials based on solid business and professional communication standards. Determine if virtual meetings are acceptable. Is e-mail the preferred medium? Does the client expect/allow text messaging? Does this particular client expect many in-person meetings, or should you send information in an e-mail to expedite the communication?

Engagement Sample Communications

Consultants produce a wide range of communications over the course of an engagement. Consulting firms typically provide templates for creating some of the output, such as progress reports or project update presentations. Other communications, particularly daily routine correspondence and reporting, may not be so prescribed. What follows here are examples of audience analyses and communications you will likely prepare during an engagement. They include:

- Project Vision Statements
- Routine E-mail Exchanges
- Significant Bad News Letters
- Engagement Instructions
- Progress Reports
- Investigative Reports

Project Vision Statements

Most engagements, simple or complex, long or short, work from a vision statement. This overarching document is something the larger project team develops, and often a consultant leads the effort. The executive sponsors might define this, though the project working team sometimes develops the vision statement. A vision statement is meant to inspire those working on the project and is a benchmark for achievement. It's also a very useful tool at the beginning of an engagement to ensure everyone is working toward the same goals. Companies also produce vision statements to inspire their employees. A project vision statement is similar but focused specifically on the activities of the project.

Here are some tips for writing a project vision statement:

- Draw up an audience analysis even for this short piece. It's focused, so it needs deliberate action.
- Write the vision as succinctly as possible so it's easy to reference throughout the project.
- Write it in the present tense and use clear language.
- Use passionate language to rally those who read it to the vision.
- Write it so it moves the project in a positive, productive direction.[7]

Exercise 3.2: Project Vision Statement

Audience Analysis:

Situation: The engagement is beginning. You need a rallying cry for the Help Desk Redesign Project.

Value: All members of the project team, from executive sponsors, to process owners, to project team members will appreciate the definition the vision creates around the work.

Purpose: The purpose is to ensure everyone understands where you're heading over the next month.

Message: The message must be upbeat and forward thinking.

Directive: The client has not asked for this, but it's a standard for most consulting engagements.

Relationship: Your relationship with the audience is still somewhat formal, and it's important to bring the client along in this communication exercise. It will be the first full project group activity, so it needs to reflect what the customer wants and what you want to deliver.

Climate and Culture: Developing this vision statement will be a delicate matter as it pushes the client to think beyond the immediate.

There may be varying views about the help desk project within the organization, and you need to bring those together as one.

Deadline: This is one of your first project tasks, and it must be completed as soon as possible. There's a possibility that bringing everyone together around a vision may take a while. You'll need to put a firm due date around this.

Product: A brief project vision statement.

Wrapper: A one-paragraph summary statement that will be incorporated into many of your project communications.

Content: The clients need to drive content as this is their vision; however, you must ensure the vision meets the contractual agreement. In this case, you will work for the next 30 days to design and deliver an implementation plan.

Organization: The statement should begin with the project's broadest goal and move toward any particular goals.

Tone: Professional and polished.

Language: Write in a simple style, using clear, direct language.

Length: One paragraph of two to three sentences.

Delivery: Once you deliver this, you will present and review it at the weekly executive sponsor meeting as well as at the weekly team meeting.

Project Vision Statement Example

Comcon Utilities seeks to provide exceptional help desk customer service by fostering a well-trained, motivated staff, using current technological assistance and streamlined processes. The Help Desk Redesign Project is dedicated to designing a plan within 30 days to launch this vision.

Routine E-mail Exchanges

As we are all aware, the proliferation of e-mail has become a management nightmare for most business people. You will most likely correspond via e-mail every day and throughout an engagement. Via e-mail, we deliver bad news and good news. We also use e-mail to instruct and inform. And while there are some communications that we still save for paper output, most of these are now often delivered via e-mail as attachments. See Appendix B for more details.

The routine e-mail exchanges that follow here are those for which the e-mail format is the preferred wrapper, not just the method of delivery. In these cases, you choose to correspond via e-mail because it is a reliable means of delivering a communication to one or multiple recipients in a timely manner. You can typically count on an e-mail being read within 24 hours, and you can usually expect a response in that period too. But while e-mails are considered part of the permanent record of an engagement, they don't usually show up in the final reports. Save those more official communications for standard correspondences like letters, memoranda, and reports. You must be clear about how and why you use e-mails, and be sure to employ other standard business correspondence media when necessary, regardless of how they are delivered.

Because you write so many e-mails, you might be tempted to let down your guard when you produce them. It is critical for a consultant to be continuously aware of this tendency. You might say something that you later regret; and by the time you realize it, your e-mail has spread to many. Whether you are in a friendly situation with a client or in a battle, whatever you write on e-mail can be volatile and affect the outcome of both your engagement and your ongoing relationship with the customer.

There's no question that e-mails are forwarded far more frequently than paper correspondence ever is. Also, because you write so much e-mail during an engagement and to so many different audiences, you can easily make a communication mistake. Exercise wisdom as to when to use e-mail and when to abandon it in favor of a face-to-face discussion. However, there's nothing more efficient than using e-mail to communicate conveniently and immediately with any number of people. By following these tips, you can effectively communicate via e-mail with both clients and your staff members during an engagement:

- Use a good subject line that clearly articulates what the reader should expect in the e-mail. If you change subjects, write a new e-mail with a new subject line.

- In the first sentence, tell readers why you're writing. Even if you need to drive toward the topic over a few sentences, remember that your readers are likely initially viewing the e-mail on a mobile device. Give them the courtesy of being able to see what the e-mail is about in the first lines visible on that device.

- Keep your e-mails on the short side. If your e-mail is long, tell the readers that early on so they can come back to it later.

- Write and edit your e-mails as you would other professional documents. Don't treat them like informal communications merely because they are written in electronic form.

- Use standard organizational methods for your e-mails. Don't ramble and use stream of consciousness just because you're not writing a formal letter.

- Address the e-mail to those individuals who must take action on the message. If you just want someone to know about the e-mail content, then copy him. Be sure, however, that those copied understand why they are receiving the e-mail. Don't just add them because you want to cover yourself.

- Don't use e-mail to vent what you should discuss in person. If someone sends you a letter of complaint, it might be best to reply and ask for a meeting, rather than continuing the rant via e-mail.

- Remember that e-mails can become public very quickly, so be discreet at all times. Engagement e-mails aren't private communications. Treat them as professionally as public discussions.

Exercise 3.3: Routine E-mail Exchange

Audience Analysis:

Situation: Your client has sent an e-mail complaining about the data you delivered at a meeting. Beyond the particular data issue, however, he has insinuated that your team doesn't know what it's doing. You must respond to that e-mail without further escalating the issue. You must also write to your analyst requesting some clarification on the data he presented before you promise too much to the client.

Value: It's important that you acknowledge the client's concerns and communicate back in a way that makes him feel as if you can move the project in a positive direction.

Purpose: Your purpose here is to stop the negative assumptions about the project from continuing.

Message: You must turn the client's opinion around and regain his confidence in your team and company.

Directive: Your client hasn't asked for a response, but it's clear you need to give one.

Relationship: Up until now, the relationship has been cooperative, but the tone of your client's e-mail is threatening.

Climate and Culture: It's not clear if this strongly worded e-mail is an accurate representation of how everyone in the meeting thinks about the project. It could indicate resistance to the project in some way, so be sure to update the project's executive sponsor. However, you probably shouldn't copy her on the e-mail back to this process owner. Tread lightly here.

Deadline: Don't answer too quickly because you may give some inaccurate or overly optimistic information just to relieve the tension.

Product: A response to this complaint.

Wrapper: You can reply via e-mail. In fact, if you reply any other way it may appear as if you are escalating the issue, which will further exacerbate the matter.

Content: Respond to the complaint but not to the specifics of the complaint since you don't know if what he purports is accurate or not. You can apologize for how he interprets the project's lack of success.

Organization: Open by apologizing for any confusion you may have caused. Then offer to investigate the matter. Close by instilling some confidence in your work.

Tone: You must be very professional, not at all emotional or personal.

Language: Your language must be confident yet humble.

Length: This is a two- to three-paragraph, brief e-mail response.

Delivery: Reply and acknowledge receipt of the e-mail on the same day, but don't include concrete answers to the allegations until you know more about the data that was presented.

Routine E-mail Exchange Example

From the client to the consultant

TO: Abigail Potter <abigail@dcs.xxx>
FROM: Les Millen <les@comcon.xxx>
SUBJECT: Disappointing Meeting Today

Abby,

Thanks for organizing today's project update meeting. I have to say that I wasn't completely satisfied with the results and expected better from your project team. Those data on our competitor's help desk metrics didn't make any sense to me. Are you sure your analyst knows what he's doing?

I'm not sure your staff thoroughly understands how our business works, and I am losing confidence in your company's ability to complete this engagement.

Let's get this project on the right track.

Les

From the consultant to the client

TO: Les Millen <les@comcon.xxx>
FROM: Abigail Potter <abigail@dcs.xxx>
SUBJECT: Disappointing Meeting Today

Dear Les,

Thank you for writing with your concerns about today's meeting and the project in general. I apologize if we didn't do a good job presenting the data we collected and analyzed on XYZ Utilities' help desk.

By tomorrow, the project team will review the data to ensure its accuracy, and I will personally report back to you on what we learn.

Are you available tomorrow morning for a chat? I'd like to discuss further the engagement details.

Thanks for your immediate feedback. We will do all we can to move forward productively.

Sincerely,

Abby

From the consultant to the data analyst

TO: Andy Solo <andy@dsc.xxx>
FROM: Abigail Potter <abigail@dcs.xxx>
SUBJECT: Immediate Attention on Data Analysis

Andy,

I'm writing to ask for your help, and I need you to confirm immediately if you can complete my request.

After this morning's meeting, I received some feedback from the executive team about the legitimacy of the metrics we provided on the XYZ help desk. Could you take another look at those data and see if there's anything you might have missed in your general analysis?

We may have to dig into this further, but it would help if you would verify by tomorrow morning that the analysis we presented is sound.

Please confirm immediately that you can review the data and respond to me by tomorrow morning. Also, please keep this communication confidential.

Thanks,

Abby

Significant Bad News Messages

As diligent as consultants and clients might be, there are periods within an engagement when things don't go as planned. Just as in all organizations, project teams encounter personnel, process, and technology issues that need resolution. A consultant is often in the unenviable position of saying "no" to a team member or, even worse, to the client. During an engagement, the client may ask for something that your firm considers out of the scope of the project. It takes composure and tact to respond appropriately. Fortunately, long-standing business communication practices exist to guide this sort of interaction.[8]

Follow this advice to deliver significant bad news: Use a formal, full-block style business letter format to deliver significant bad news. This includes corresponding on company letterhead with a signature (electronic is acceptable).

- If you determine to send the letter via e-mail, attach it to the e-mail. Do not write the letter within an e-mail text box.
- Begin the letter with a goodwill statement, but tell the writer why you are writing early in the first paragraph of the letter.
- Detail the circumstances around the bad news then state your decision or rejection.
- End your letter with a goodwill closing that looks ahead.
- Use professional, respectful business language.
- Apologize for any wrongdoing but only once in the letter.

Exercise 3.4: Significant Bad News

Audience Analysis:

Situation: Your project is delayed by 10 days because of a lack of decision data. You met with the company executive but now must put the delay in writing.

Value: The client wants this incident in writing for contractual reasons, so you must detail the problem and take responsibility for the delay.

Purpose: The purpose of this piece is to inform the client of the project delay but also instill confidence in final project completion.

Message: You're delivering bad news, so write a formal business letter.

Directive: The client has requested the letter to document the bad news delivered at a meeting.

Relationship: The relationship with your client is harmonious, but this is a turning point since you are not delivering as agreed.

Climate and Culture: The project team has been working tirelessly, and this is its first major setback. You need to instill confidence in the client that you can deliver the plan, even though it will be late.

Deadline: You need to send this letter to the client by the end of business today, as she requested.

Product: This is a letter delivering bad news and promising an adjustment.

Wrapper: This should be in a formal, full-block style correspondence.

Content: Include the classic bad news by stating the problem and the reasons for it and by issuing an apology.

Organization: Follow the formal method of delivering bad news.

Tone: Your tone must be extremely professional, humble, yet confident.

Language: Language must be clear and detailed. Only promise what you can deliver so that matters don't escalate.

Length: This is a brief one-page letter.

Delivery: Send a cover e-mail to your client, with the formal letter attached.

Significant Bad News Letter Example

Diversified Consulting Services, Inc.
123 S. Main Street
Chester, VT 03257

February 20, 2017

Ms. Janet Mercurion
Executive Director for User Services
Comcon Utilities
140 Bridgetown Street
New Haven, CT 02395

Dear Ms. Mercurion:

Thank you for meeting with my team last week to dis- | Congenial
cuss the status of the Help Desk Redesign Project. We | opening with
have made considerable progress in a short period, and | alert
we remain confident that we will be able to produce a
viable implementation plan to support the significant
improvements to your help desk operation. We have,
however, recently experienced some obstacles, and we
are writing to report that we will not be able to meet
our final report deadline of March 1, 2017.

As you know, the team, made up of members of your | Circumstances
staff and our consultants and analysts, has worked | leading to bad
diligently to complete the research and planning | news
needed to design an implementation plan. We have
interviewed all Comcon help desk staff members and
reviewed all support processes. We have also been able
to survey the help desk support technologies available
on the market. We have not, however, been able to
evaluate your current customer service metrics confidently, and we need those data to make our final
recommendations.

We are confident that by March 1, 2017, we will have | Recommended
completed our data analysis and woven the knowledge | next steps—
from those analytics into our plan. We expect to be | action plan
able to present a final report to the executive team by
March 10, 2017. Please accept our apology for this
delay. We remain committed to providing Comcon
with a viable implementation plan for its redesign of
user help desk services.

Thank you for your continued support.

Sincerely,

James D. Cowens

James D. Cowens
President

Engagement Instructions

Consultants constantly write instructions. During an engagement, you will issue dozens of directives to both your own team and the clients. For example, you may need to instruct your client on how to document a business process or how to use the project's data management systems. Since time is of the essence, and because there are many people involved during an engagement, it makes good sense to write these instructions, even if they are very simple ones. Don't assume your client or team members know what you know, what you want, or how you want it done. As you gain more experience as a consultant, you may quickly forget how intimidating and confusing the world of an engagement might be from the perspective of the various involved parties.

Instructions can be written within the context of an e-mail, a memorandum, or a letter. They can also stand alone and be sent to your audience with a brief cover letter or note. The specifics depend on the situation at hand and should be determined when you analyze the audience. Everyone encounters frustrating instructions and has a tale to tell about trying to follow them only to fail. Ironically, instructions are easy to write, but you should be aware of a few standards that make them more digestible and effective:

- Organize your instructions in sequential order, exactly the way someone should do the work.
- Write the instructions in simple steps.
- Use clear and direct language and vocabulary.
- Use transitions to move from one step to the next.
- Write each step as a command and in the active voice.
- Insert visuals if they help make your words clearer.

- Be sure to alert your audience to any warnings or possible problems.
- Test the instructions.
- Use the same formatting/template for all instructional communications throughout the project.

Exercise 3.5: Engagement Instructions

Audience Analysis:

Situation: You will be away from the project for a day when there is much work scheduled. One of your consulting team members, Peter, will manage the work of the teams today but has not done this in the past. Write him with some instructions so he can direct the teams and not lose momentum.

Value: Peter, your colleague, needs solid instructions to be able to perform this task.

Purpose: Your purpose is to direct Peter, so your teams continue to work at full force in your absence.

Message: You are asking for a professional favor and must provide necessary information.

Directive: Provide details though no one has asked for these instructions.

Relationship: Peter has a congenial relationship with you. If you're detailed, he'll follow your instructions to the letter.

Climate and Culture: You need to put Peter in a good position to do this work as the clients will become impatient and lose interest if he can't coordinate their work.

Deadline: Send these instructions to Peter before his day begins and with enough time to ask any questions.

Product: Writing a set of instructions for each team.

Wrapper: This will be a set of instructions in an e-mail.

Content: Include enough information so Peter knows what the work is and where to find information.

Organization: Organize these instructions by team and then tasks.

Tone: Write this professionally but not too formally.

Language: Write clearly and directly, being as precise as possible without overprescribing every step.

Length: These instructions won't be too long, perhaps one page.

Delivery: Write these in an e-mail since this is a routine transaction and will not become a formal piece of the engagement documentation.

Engagement Instructions Example

TO: Peter Jordan <peter@dsc.xxx>
FROM: Abigail Potter <abigail@dcs.xxx>
SUBJECT: Instructions for Today's Activities with the Comcon Project Team

Hi Peter,

Thanks for being willing to cover for me today on the daily activities with the project team. I thought I'd document the series of activities I had planned for the group and how to undertake them. I've organized the work according to team assignments.

Specific request

Instructions for Organization Redesign Team:

- Complete the interviews with all employees.
- Document major issues which emerged from the interviews. (Do this on the spreadsheet.)
- Review and update organizational charts.

Instructions written as "commands" and organized by topic area

Instructions for Process Redesign Team:

- Direct process redesign team members to present their cases.

- Video-record each of the presentations and file them in our project folder labeled "Process Videos."
- E-mail each team member who presented his or her video and ask them to make comments on the video board. (You can find this board in our project folder labeled "Process Videos.")

Instructions for Technology Process Redesign Team:

- Ask the technology team members to send you any updates on their market study.
- File any new technology company product briefs in our project folder labeled "Company Briefs."

These activities should be more than enough for each team to accomplish today. If you have any problems with any of this information or if new matters emerge, you can text me at any point today. I may be in meetings, but I'll get back to you as soon as possible.

"What if" scenarios to support reader

Thanks again, Peter.

Abby

Progress Reports

Progress reports are the backbone of any engagement or project. Project plans inform all parties what will happen when. However, sponsors and managers want to hear directly from consultants how a project has been going and what is left to be completed. During an engagement, these updates often occur in person during regularly scheduled meetings, but it's also a good idea to document progress, especially for executive sponsors. These brief reports help managers and executives keep up to date on a regular basis. They inform executives about activities, budgets, and schedule at a level high enough to involve them in the engagement's progress. However, they don't drill down into details; those are held in the project plan.

Sending progress reports to engagement personnel can also support a project's long-term success. When the client can follow the project from week to week via a progress report, for example, she knows of any areas of concern far in advance and can potentially mitigate issues and help steer her staff. She can also support you as the consultant better by working with you to keep the project on track.

From a business communication strategy perspective, progress reports are considered informal reports. You can include them within the context of an e-mail, a memorandum, or a letter. They can also be written as a standalone report and sent with a cover letter. In a consulting engagement, they are typically prepared for the executive sponsor. That sponsor may ask you for the report as part of the contract, or you may just decide it's a good idea to prepare one and send it. The following guidelines will support you when writing progress reports:

- Include the date range for which progress is being reported.
- Immediately tell the reader the overall status of the engagement regarding activities, schedule, and budget.
- If there are significant problems, tell this to the reader in the first few sentences. You can go into detail about these problems later in the report.
- Organize your report around what has been accomplished and what work still needs to be done.
- Do not go into detail about what you have uncovered during the engagement. You are reporting on the engagement's progress, not on the engagement's topic.
- Tell the reader the nature of the problems the engagement is encountering and detail a plan for resolution and the date by which you expect to have a plan.
- End the report by asking for any specific information or direction you need to move ahead with the project.
- Tell the reader when she can expect the next engagement progress report.

Exercise 3.6: Progress Report

Audience Analysis:

Situation: This is the third week of your consulting engagement, and you need to update your executive sponsor on your progress. This is the third of the updates you have been sending weekly. However, this time, you must report a problem that may delay the engagement's completion.

Value: The value for both you and the client. This update allows the client to know where the engagement stands and what is left to be completed. For you, the value is that the client can closely follow any issues or risks you are encountering that she may help mitigate.

Purpose: Your purpose is to update your executive sponsor on this week's project status.

Message: Your message is a routine update.

Directive: Your executive sponsor expects this update once a week, so she will look for it and compare it to the previous week's report.

Relationship: You are the lead consultant on this engagement writing to your executive sponsor. This is formal.

Climate and Culture: The project has been going well up until this point, but you have encountered a major obstacle that threatens the engagement's timeline. You need to express this openly without creating a crisis. You'll need to include a meeting request so you can meet face to face soon after she reads this report.

Deadline: You will send this on your regular weekly schedule, but only because that is tomorrow and you just learned the scheduling problems news today.

Product: This is a progress report.

Wrapper: You will write this progress report within a letter format as it is a formal piece of project documentation from the consulting firm to the client.

Content: Include work that you've completed and the work scheduled. Report on the overall status of the project, in this case with a notation about the problem encountered and its impact on the timeline for completion.

Organization: Open the letter with an overall status statement. Next, present a summary of the work completed and the work scheduled. End with a plan to meet as you know she will want to do that.

Tone: Be formal and professional as this is to your client sponsor.

Language: Use language that is clear and direct. The audience needs to know exactly what the problem is that you've encountered and what is necessary to get back on track.

Length: This progress report, like your others, will be one to one and a half pages long.

Delivery: You will send this letter attached to an e-mail, as you want the speedy electronic delivery but need the formal letter to be intact outside of e-mail format.

Progress Report Example

Diversified Consulting Services, Inc.

123 S. Main Street

Chester, VT 03257

February 12, 2017

Ms. Janet Mercurion   Formal letter

Executive Director for User Services   format to

Comcon Utilities   external client

140 Bridgetown Street

New Haven, CT 02395

Re: Help Desk Redesign Project Progress Report week   Period of

of 2/10/17   Progress

Dear Ms. Mercurion:

We are writing to update you on the Help Desk Rede-   Overall status
sign Project engagement. The engagement is on bud-
get and moving forward, but we have encountered
some scheduling difficulties that may make it necessary to extend our project completion date.

Work Accomplished

Work
completed by
topic area

Team Formation:

All team members have on-boarded to the project and have received the training necessary to
perform their redesign tasks.

Organizational Redesign:

The organization design team has completed all
its interviews with staff members and reviewed
all organizational materials and charts.

Process Redesign Team:

The process design team has documented exist-
ing processes and begun to analyze help desk
data where available.

Work Scheduled

Work
completed by
date

Weeks of February 12 and 19

- Create new organizational charts and job
  descriptions for new positions.
- Complete creation of new process designs.

Weeks of February 26 and March 4

- Finalize data analysis of competitor metrics.
- Complete final report

March 10*

- Deliver final report to Help Desk Redesign
  Executive Team

*As you know, we were scheduled to complete all work   Meeting
and deliver the final report on March 1. However, we   request to
are currently running behind on our data analysis of   move forward

the Help Desk metrics. We now estimate March 10 as our completion date.

Please let me know as soon as possible how we should address this schedule change. I will call your assistant to schedule a time for us to discuss this unanticipated change and its ramifications for the engagement.

Thank you for your continued support.

Sincerely,

Abigail Potter

Abigail Potter
Senior Consultant

Investigative Reports

Most engagements revolve around gathering data, analyzing it, drawing conclusions, and making recommendations. An engagement is typically organized into these categories, and the consultant and his team conclude with a primary presentation or formal report to the client sponsors. In business communication terms that report is characterized as an investigative report.

Investigative reports can be informal or formal, and they can be solicited or unsolicited. Formal investigative reports have a very specialized format that includes all materials surrounding the broader engagement.[9] They are typically written at the conclusion of an engagement and form the permanent record of all activities. The client does not necessarily solicit one, but there is an expectation that the engagement will conclude with a report.

Informal investigative reports also find their way into engagements. They are less formal in that they don't prescribe a particular format, but they do include some standard information. They can be included as part of an e-mail or in a memorandum. They can also be found as standalone reports covered by a letter. This is especially the case in a shorter, less complex engagement when the client asks a consultant for an investigation and a written summary report. In a more complex engagement, the consultant and project members often gather subsets of information. They then create a slide presentation and a shorter investigative report reflecting what they have gathered. The conclusions and recommendations in these informal investigative reports often make their way into the formal final engagement report.

It's useful for you as a consultant to know how to plan, organize, and write informal investigative reports because they are useful not only in expressing recommendations but in logically bringing forth new information to a client. For less complex engagements, an informal investigative report can be an appropriate deliverable to conclude a project. The following guidelines will help you organize and prepare an informal investigative report:

- Determine the most appropriate way, based on your audience, to present the report (in an e-mail, in a memorandum, or as a standalone report with a cover letter).
- Use lists, bullet points, and bold typeface where appropriate so your reader can reference your detail easily. Don't expect readers to thoroughly study the entire report.
- Introduce the investigation topic. If the reader has asked for the report, you can move into the investigation after a simple statement of purpose. If the reader has not asked for the report, you should give more background that led to the purpose of the investigation.
- Tell the reader the scope of your investigation. How broadly did you study the topic?
- Report your findings. Organizing these by subject headings is useful.
- State any logical conclusions you draw from the findings.
- If appropriate, make recommendations or suggest next steps based on your logical conclusions.[10]

Exercise 3.7: Investigative Report

Audience Analysis:

Situation: You conducted a study of current help desk software on the market to inform your project team of those systems that should be considered as part of the implementation plan.

Value: The value to the audience is to understand best what currently exists in the market and to give some factual details about what software to purchase.

Purpose: The purpose of this report is to inform the project team and the executive sponsors of currently available software that might meet Comcon's help desk needs.

Message: This is an engagement-critical piece as it provides a significant recommendation.

Directive: The lead consultant and the executive sponsor team have requested this.

Relationship: You are in the middle of the engagement and are writing to the project team. You are writing to two readers; one represents your consulting company while the other represents your client. The piece will be formal because it will be a permanent piece of the engagement record.

Climate and Culture: All readers are looking forward to these results. Write the report as an internal communication since you are working together on the engagement; there is no need to write a letter as an outside consultant.

Deadline: Deliver this report earlier than when you will present. You must gain a review and approval of the recommendations before you give the final project report now scheduled for March 1.

Product: This will be an informal investigative report.

Wrapper: Write the report as an internal memorandum but with the components of an investigative report.

Content: Include the overall summary of findings, but do not provide all the detail in this report. For example, refer to the user and technical requirements, but don't provide the detail of the requirements. That information will be available within the project documentation, but it is not appropriate for this audience.

Organization: Organize the standard investigative report content including purpose, scope, findings, conclusions, and recommendations.

Tone: Keep your tone professional.

Language: Language will be clear and direct with no techno-speak.

Length: The report will probably be one to two pages long, based on the level of detail.

Delivery: E-mail this report to the lead engagement consultant and the help desk process owner and expect that it will be forwarded to the executive sponsors. You will write the report as a separate memorandum but attach it to an e-mail for further distribution.

Investigative Report Example

MEMORANDUM

TO: Abby Potter, Senior Consultant, DCS, Inc.
          Walter Smart, Help Desk Manager, Comcon Utilities
FROM: Peter Jordan, Help Desk Redesign Expert, DCS, Inc.
          John Wilkins, Comcon Help Desk Technology Manager,
          Comcon Utilities
DATE: February 1, 2017
SUBJECT: Help Desk Support Software Market Review

As requested, we led an investigation into the current help desk technologies available on the market. We're writing to report our findings and to make recommendations for which companies will be sent a Request for Proposal.

Purpose of Investigation

As part of the Comcon Utilities Help Desk Redesign Project, the project team has determined that a new call tracking system is required.

The current Comcon system, Can I Help You, was implemented 10 years ago. Can I Help You tracks basic call data, but it is outdated. Current problems include:

- Lack of escalation tracking
- Poor metrics tracking
- Old server-based technology
- Infrequent upgrades
- Limited maximum user allowance (15)
- Inadequate predictive analytics capability

Scope of Investigation

The Help Desk Redesign Project Technology Task Force reviewed materials on four currently popular software products that specialize or have expertise in the communication utilities call tracking. These included:

- Can I Help You Too
- Communications Call Power
- Problem Tracker
- Know Your Issues

We reviewed the products based on the following criteria:

- Comcon user requirements
- Comcon technical requirements
- Software infrastructure model
- Client usage and references

Summary of Findings

All products are currently operating at major communication utilities call center and help desk operations. They have all upgraded their technology architecture to modern standards and are routinely applying enhancements to the products. By product, our findings include:

Can I Help You Too

This is the upgraded version of the software Comcon currently uses in support of its help desk. The new product meets 90% of our user requirements and 70% of our defined technical requirements. It is cloud computing based and charges by the number of annual calls. It distinguishes itself by its advanced used of mobile technology to both make and accept calls. It also provides full data conversion from Can I Help You customers.

Communications Call Power

This is the oldest product reviewed. It meets 60% of our user specifications and 40% of our technical requirements. It is server based and charges an annual software license fee based on usage. It distinguishes itself by having the largest installed base of all the products reviewed.

Problem Tracker

This is the newest product on the market. It meets 90% of both our user and technical requirements. It offers a server or cloud-based option. It distinguishes itself as having a strong management tool module and a user-friendly interface.

Know Your Issues

This product focuses more on issue management than on a user-friendly interface. It meets 75% of our user requirements and 80% of our technical requirements. If offers server or cloud-based options. It distinguishes itself by offering robust analytics and follow through metrics.

Conclusions

Based on these findings, Comcon should further investigate three of the four products. Comcon should consider Can I Help You Too, Problem Tracker, and Know Your Issues. Communications Call Power does not substantially meet Comcon's user or technical requirements.

Can I Help You Too may be a good option for closer examination. It is the only system that would allow Comcon to convert previous data into the new software.

Recommendations

The Help Desk Redesign Project Technology Task Force recommends the following next steps:

- Issue RFP requests to Can I Help You Too, Problem Tracker, and Know Your Issues.
- Perform preliminary reference checks on the three products.
- Meet with the Comcon Can I Help You Too account representative to understand product direction and conversion possibilities.

Thank you for the opportunity to study and report on this matter. Please let us know if we can provide more details or if you have any questions. We look forward to presenting these results at our next executive sponsor update.

Chapter Conclusion

A consultant's work is at the heart of the engagement. Whether you are the lead consultant who is managing an engagement or you play a supporting role, this is where you live. An engagement might run from one day to many years; regardless, it is broken down into tasks, milestones, and an outcome. Around all of this work, consultants communicate. They communicate with one another, with client representatives, and within and outside of teams.

As an engagement progresses, new working groups form and relationships change. Your client who once was a stranger now becomes the colleague, working toward the same objectives and goals. Even though new alliances are forged, you must remain clear about the role you play and the value your communication has. You will generate a wide variety of routine correspondence, reports, presentations, and other materials. Each time you produce one of these, take the time to analyze your audience for high impact that will ensure your engagement's success.

CHAPTER 4

Post-Engagement Communication

In this chapter, we turn our attention to the post-engagement phase and what a consultant's role is in communications during this period. Post-engagement begins as soon as the final contractual obligations are completed, and it goes on as long as the consulting services firm and the client interact.

Here we will:

- review types of communication during this phase,
- detail the environment from both a consultant and a client's perspective,
- analyze the audience during post-engagement and essential communications, and
- consider tips for writing and presenting post-engagement communications.

The Post-Engagement Phase

Just as in the pre-engagement phase, a consultant moves to the sidelines during post-engagement. The work of the project is done, and account managers typically take the lead in following up with the client on any next steps. As we have seen in the pre-engagement phase, effective consultants are wise to follow what transpires after an engagement and may contribute to presentations and reports.

The post-engagement phase is the period when your company completes an engagement. Relationships change yet again as working teams separate, clients on teams return to their full-time jobs, and consultants are redeployed to other projects. There is a natural and necessary parting of the ways. Most of your firm's communication revolves around pro-posing possible additional business opportunities. The communication is formal and congenial.

The Post-Engagement Communication

In this book, we have established three separate phases within which we are analyzing communication. In reality, there is a blurred line when moving across stages. For example, an engagement may officially end on the day of the final report presentation. But, in reality, the relationship, thus the engagement, doesn't just abruptly end. Everyone involved ties up loose ends. And there are many opportunities for the consulting firm or independent consultant to continue communicating with the client.

In many ways, after an engagement, the relationship goes back to the way it was before the engagement. You have services to offer and the client may or may not want to buy those services. Your communications, then, are much the way they were before the engagement. Much informal communication occurs. Your client and your firm's representatives meet one-on-one in office sessions, at luncheons, and on the phone. However, there is also an amount of more formal business communication that can go on, especially if there is an opportunity to provide more services.

Let's turn our attention to some possible post-engagement communications.

Correspondence and Documentation

As the engagement winds down and concludes, you or your firm might initiate several letters or e-mails to the client. You may also complete proj-ect documentation at this point. Here are several examples:

Project completion letters: You or someone from your firm may write a letter to the client expressing gratitude for the opportunity to do business.

Add-on services sales letters: The principal engagement manager or account manager may write to the customer putting forth suggestions to provide add-on services. You may be asked to contribute, as the consul-tant who best understands what add-on services might be required after the engagement. If you are an independent consultant, you may write these yourself soon after an engagement ends.

Project plan completion: At this stage, the project plans need updating and finalization. You or your project manager, if there is one, ensures that the plans are updated and reflect the activities and schedule that were planned and the actual outcome. These, along with any reports, correspondence, schedules and documentation, are passed along to the client's internal project manager. If you're a new consultant, you may want to keep copies (barring any confidentiality or contractual issues) of project documentation as samples for future engagements. Your firm keeps a copy as a permanent record.

Post-Implementation Presentations and Reports

Add-on services presentation: It is likely that your engagement manager or account representative will request a follow-up meeting with the client executives. The focus of this presentation is to advise the client on what services you can extend to further the work done during the engagement. You will likely contribute to this since you're aware of what next steps would be appropriate.

Post-implementation review (PIR) client report: Consultants often perform PIRs after an engagement is completed. Clients may ask for this as part of the original engagement contract or as an add-on service. In either case, the report is a summary of what you study, conclude, and recommend about the engagement project. As part of the PIR, you and your project team evaluate what you did during the engagement and what could have been improved. You also target additional opportunities for furthering the objectives of the original project.

Examples and tips for writing various types of engagement communications are located at the end of this chapter.

The Post-Engagement Environment

Once the engagement is over, your writing and presenting to the client will revert to being more formal, as it was during pre-engagement. In fact, as a consultant, you won't interact with the client at all unless you do that at the request of your manager. If you are an independent consultant, you'll shift your focus away from any process owner interactions and back to your executive sponsors.

The environmental conditions once again influence your audience analysis and resulting communications.

What the Consultant Brings to the Environment

After an engagement, you will have a great sense of accomplishment and completion. Regardless of any obstacles you and your colleagues may have faced, you likely have completed your tasks and delivered a quality product to your client. Once you wrap up all the documentation and make your final presentations, you close the door on the engagement. You may even move on to a new assignment after wrapping up some loose ends.

Ironically, you have now become an expert of the sort your client hoped for in the first place. You might have brought valuable experience and knowledge when you walked into the engagement, but in post-engagement, you are also an expert on the topics you investigated during the engagement. Your general expertise has transformed into very specific knowledge about some of the workings of your client's operations. You know how much your firm accomplished and what might have been out of scope but that should have happened. That knowledge is extremely valuable both to your company and to your client. You may have closed the door on the engagement, but your firm has probably not done so. Additionally, your client probably still needs help to move forward.

Post-implementation is, then, a period of high hopes and possibility. You may be asked to contribute once again, this time to sales proposals and PIRs. You may even approach the client for a new engagement and the cycle starts all over again.

How the Client Comes to the Environment

As we've discussed, the engagement and post-engagement phases are typically filled with the possibility of change and improvement. If your engagement has been successful, your client won't want to see you go. If the engagement hasn't been successful, your client firm will want you to fix what you didn't deliver to their satisfaction. Either way, there will be some separation anxiety at this point and there should be.

POST-ENGAGEMENT COMMUNICATION   95

Post-engagement is often a tumultuous time for the client who is left to carry out the work you left behind. If, for example, your final report recommended a new organization, a new technology, or a new set of processes, your client is left to implement the change. Many of the expectations, assumptions, and emotions that the client had in pre-engagement also re-emerge at this point. Without active client executive sponsorship and clear next steps, work tends to go back to the way it was before the engagement. Sometimes clients experience burnout and need a break. They have been doing two jobs, the work of the engagement and their everyday work, for an extended period. Priorities might change for the client organization, and the engagement work may be put on hold. It's also possible that the vision created during the engagement may erode in your absence. Finally, perhaps you will find that not everything happened that you and your team planned during the engagement.

All of this unfinished business creates an opportunity for your firm and your client. Your communication during post-engagement should reflect the positive possibilities.

Post-Engagement Audience Analysis

Throughout this book, we have focused on how to approach your audience and its needs. Just as we explored in the pre-engagement and engagement phases, post-engagement has its set of audience peculiarities. During this period of opportunity, excellent communication can make a positive impact on your audience and enhance your relationship even further than it did during the engagement period. Keeping a clear purpose, appropriate content, tone, language, and format continues to drive your communication during post-engagement.

Use the following post-engagement audience analysis when you create your own.

Exercise 4.1: Post-engagement

Audience Analysis:

Situation: The post-engagement period immediately follows the engagement's completion. You have provided all contractual obligations and deliverables.

Value: Your client will only value information and ideas that further the work of the engagement, especially immediately after it ends. If you're selling new services, you'll need to present your recommendations and then back into details. Your audience will want you to be very conscious of their time constraints.

Purpose: This will depend on the specific communication.

Message: This will depend on the specific communication. However, during post-engagement, your message will focus less on operational matters and more on strategy for moving forward.

Directive: You are most likely presenting your firm's standard materials during post-engagement. You may write or present as a result of a direct request from the client. Regardless, be aware of how much detail you include or exclude at this point.

Relationship: Your relationship with your client is once again quite formal and professional, and your communication should mirror that. You know each other well since you've been through an engagement together; however, that should not change the level of formality in your communication. This is a time for new business. You also know each other's communication styles and the material you're discussing, so you might be able to refer to some details without providing much background.

Climate and Culture: Since you've worked with this client for a while, you should already know what acceptable communication standards are. Remind yourself of these.

Deadline: This will depend on the specific communication.

Product: Regardless of what you are delivering in this communication, your written output must be extremely professional and lean to the formal. If you're making a presentation, you can be somewhat less formal.

Wrapper: This will depend on the specific communication; however, you should follow client protocols if possible and bring materials in from the engagement when possible.

Content: Be very aware of how much your audience members know about the engagement. If the engagement has just ended, most of your audience will be aware of the specifics you'll discuss. However, if there are new players at the client site, it's important that you're as detailed and inclusive as possible, or you risk losing these new audience members.

Organization: You are likely offering add-on services during this phase. Present the material so that your audience absorbs it quickly and easily. The client is not likely to be as patient and eager as when you were in the pre-engagement and engagement periods.

Tone: Your tone must be professional and cordial. You can be somewhat familiar but not informal. This is new business.

Language: Your language must not contain any corporate jargon or project specific language that your audience doesn't understand. Be especially aware of this issue with new client representatives.

Length: This will depend on the specific communication.

Delivery: You'll need to know how your client typically delivers information and follow that. You'll have to determine if virtual meetings are acceptable. Is e-mail the preferred medium? Does the client expect/allow text messaging? Does this particular client expect many in-person meetings, or should you send information in an e-mail to expedite the communication?

Post-Engagement Sample Communications

Just as we described in the pre-engagement period, as a consultant, you are not likely to take the communications lead during post-engagement. The engagement is over, and what might have become a very relaxed relationship may still be that; but the context of the communication once again takes on a more formal and professional tone.

You will contribute to at least two post-engagement communications. The work of the engagement is over, but the client information you have gained is invaluable for future endeavors. The following two examples will help you create communications that support your client's post-engagement success:

- PIR report
- Add-on services sales letter

Post Implementation Review Client Report

As part of standard project management protocol, teams review and analyze the work completed and document what went well and what could have been improved upon. The entire PIR results are usually internal data reserved for your company. The focus of the overall PIR is to evaluate how well your firm accomplished its objectives in delivering to the client and how it can improve on other similar projects in the future. PIRs assess a number of elements: how well the project outcomes mirror the original objectives; if the goals of the project were met; if the client is satisfied; what else could be implemented to improve the situation; if the project was on time and budget; and what could go better the next time a similar project is undertaken.[1]

Lessons learned from the PIR process can also make their way into a report for the client. In the client version of the PIR report, the focus is more on whether the client objectives were met and if the client is satisfied with how well the project ran. Incorporate the following when you produce a client PIR report:

- Use the investigative report guidelines examined in Chapter 3 as a basis for your document. The PIR is a type of investigation.
- Focus on the value to the client. Clients want to know more about what you did well for the company than how well you think you ran your project.
- Include a balanced and open view of the effectiveness of the engagement in meeting the client's objectives.
- When possible, include metrics to support your claims.
- Use report-formatting techniques such as headings, bulleted lists, and bold typeface to make your report readable and easy to reference.

- State your conclusions and recommendations succinctly so they can quickly turn into next steps for additional engagement opportunities.

Exercise 4.2: Post Implementation Review Client Report

Audience Analysis:

Situation: At the conclusion of the Help Desk Redesign Project at Comcon, you conducted an internal PIR to evaluate the project outcomes. You now want to report back to the client on the opportunities you discovered that can create additional value added for her and her team.

Value: The value to the audience is to understand what you were able to accomplish but also what you can additionally provide to solidify the client's ongoing success.

Purpose: The purpose of this report is to inform the client of additional services you can provide based on the information gathered in the PIR.

Message: You are delivering good news. You were able to complete the project and provide the client with a reliable implementation plan that will help Comcon improve its help desk services.

Directive: Your client has not requested this, so you need to set the context of why the information is valuable.

Relationship: Your relationship with the client is excellent and you delivered what you promised. However, you're not sure the client wants to pay for any additional outside consultation so you need to focus on your value-added services.

Climate and Culture: Most of the client process owners were happy with the engagement outcome and would like to do business with you again. However, one process owner has been critical of your involvement. If possible, you need to avoid any of his trigger points.

Deadline: There is no deadline for this. The information is current since you completed the project one month ago. Also, the principal parties are all still working at Comcon so it's best to send this report and ask for a meeting now before any management turnover occurs.

Product: This will be an informal investigative report.

Wrapper: Write the report to include the elements of an investigative report but as a standalone so it can be distributed.

Content: Include an overall summary of findings, conclusions, and recommendations. Don't give all the detail of your internal PIR but include those elements that the client considers valuable for her company's objectives.

Organization: Organize the standard investigative report content, including purpose, scope, findings, conclusions, and recommendations.

Tone: Your tone should be professional.

Language: Your language will be clear and direct. Don't include any techno-speak.

Length: The report will probably be one to two pages long based on the level of detail.

Delivery: E-mail this report so it arrives as soon as possible, but attach it to the email with a formal business cover letter. Also, send a paper version of the letter and report and coordinate its delivery the same day as the e-mail arrives.

Post Implementation Review Client Report Example

**COMCON UTILITIES HELP DESK REDESIGN PROJECT
POST IMPLEMENTATION REVIEW CLIENT REPORT
APRIL 1, 2017**

Background

In February 2017, Diversified Consulting Services, Inc. was engaged by Comcon Utilities to lead a cross-functional team to redesign its help desk operation. From February 1 until March 15, the Help Desk Redesign Project Team made up of DCS consultants and specialists worked closely with Comcon process owners and subject matter experts to review the current state of the organization, processes, and technology that support the help desk operation.

The project team expressed its main objectives in the following vision statement:

> Comcon Utilities seeks to provide exceptional help desk customer service by fostering a well-trained, motivated staff, using current technological assistance and streamlined processes. The Help Desk Redesign Project is dedicated to designing a plan within 30 days to launch this vision.

On March 10, the project team delivered its high-level implementation plan for the redesign. The plan calls for the implementation of the Help Desk redesign processes, the formation of a new organization, and the purchase of a new issue tracking system.

Post Implementation Review

After the engagement, DCS, Inc. and Comcon help desk staffs have critically reviewed what the project team accomplished. They have also identified gaps in the process and targeted areas for additional development.

This report reflects the results of the PIR as it relates to opportunities for Comcon to move forward with the recommended plan.

Within the three major categories, the project team studied and evaluated, several major implementation recommendations emerged.

Process Redesign Implementation

- Implement the new process design for all call tracking and escalation.
- Institute periodic target metrics for call tracking.
- Design and implement data analytics reporting for call tracking and follow through.

Organizational Redesign

- Establish a new organization structure to support the help desk unit.
- Redesign current help desk front line positions.
- Create a new management structure for issue tracking.

Technology Redesign

- Issue a Request for Proposal for a new tracking system.

PIR Identified Areas of Opportunity

As a result of the PIR process, the project team has identified areas that now need attention for Comcon to take advantage of the work begun in the Help Desk Redesign Project.

These areas of opportunity include:

Process Redesign

- Pilot the new call tracking and escalation process running parallel to the old process.
- Build the analytics reporting system for call tracking and escalation.
- Implement the target metrics for call tracking within the pilot.

Organizational Redesign

- Design new management and support organization.
- Perform a market review of new positions and classify jobs.
- Evaluate current staff expertise and performance. Slot current staff into new positions. Identify staffing gaps and advertise positions, as necessary.
- Develop and deploy a staff training program, short and long term.

Technology Redesign

- Send RFPs to recommended help desk systems vendors.
- Organize vendor demonstrations.
- Organize product selection process.
- Implement new system.

Next Step Recommendations

Based on these areas of opportunities identified through the PIR, the Help Desk Redesign Project Team recommends the following.

- Establish an internal Comcon Help Desk Redesign Implementation Team led by a Comcon manager.
- Secure external support to oversee the implementation of the areas of opportunity detailed.

Add-on Services Sales Letter

Engagement managers, account managers, and even consultants often write sales letters in the post-engagement period. As an engagement closes out, there are many opportunities for an independent consultant or a consulting firm to propose additional services. For example, we just reviewed the outcome of a PIR, the process by which you identify the effectiveness of the engagement with an eye toward the future. Your company would send an add-on services sales letter following that report. This sales letter would combine several messages:

- A goodwill reminder of the good work that the client and your company have accomplished together.
- A reference to further opportunities that have already been identified.
- A request to meet to discuss further options.

Exercise 4.3: Add-on Services Sales Letter

Audience Analysis:

Situation: You have just completed a PIR at Comcon. You're writing to your client to suggest some additional consulting services and to request a meeting to discuss the possibilities.

Value: Your executive sponsor will be interested in moving the implementation of the Help Desk Redesign ahead. You need to focus on suggesting add-on services that will accomplish this.

Purpose: Your purpose is to sell additional consulting services.

Message: You are delivering both good and bad news. The good news is that the engagement was successful and there are other opportunities. The client might consider it bad news to suggest additional outside services to complete the implementation.

Product: You're writing a sales/proposal letter and making a meeting request.

Content: Include the general services you can provide and expected outcomes.

Organization: Organize the letter by first reporting on the PIR and then move to the meeting request.

Tone: Your tone will be professional, friendly, and cordial. This client knows you well.

Language: Be specific enough to gain her interest in meeting with you but general enough so as not to promise any specifics.

Length: This will be a one-page letter. Be respectful of your client's time.

Delivery: You can send this via e-mail but the letter should be written in a formal business style so it can be attached.

Add-on Services Sales Letter Example

Diversified Consulting Services, Inc.
123 S. Main Street
Chester, VT 03257

April 10, 2017

Ms. Janet Mercurion
Executive Director for User Services
Comcon Utilities
140 Bridgetown Street
New Haven, CT 02395

Formal letter to external client with cordial opening

Dear Ms. Mercurion:

Thank you again for your support during our recent engagement on the Help Desk Process Redesign Project. It was a pleasure working with you and your team, and we are delighted to have the opportunity now to discuss providing additional services for Comcon, specifically for your help desk unit.

The redesign report we supplied you with on March 10, 2017 established a solid blueprint from which Comcon can improve its help desk organization. As you know, the project team, made up of your staff and our consultants, recently conducted a PIR of the project. The PIR returned very favorable results with much opportunity for advancement.

Context for letter

Diversified Consulting Services, Inc. is poised to help Comcon through the implementation phase. We would like to offer our services to respond to the PIR next step recommendations. Specifically, we can support Comcon in this next phase by:

Add-on sales details

- Advising the internal implementation team on the PIR recommended next steps.
- Developing the analytics reports and implementing the metrics.
- Overseeing the RFP and vendor selection process to purchase the new help desk call tracking system.
- Assisting the redesign and implementation of all organizational matters, including position reclassification and staff training.

Our recent work for Comcon and our overall experience in the help desk field makes us particularly valuable to you and your team. We can help you implement the proposed plan effectively and efficiently with minimal disruption to your team.

Why your company should do this work

We'd like the opportunity to discuss this in person. Do   Meeting
you think we could meet in the next week to discuss   request
next step possibilities?

Thanks so much, Janet, for your business.

Sincerely,

James D. Cowens

James D. Cowens
President

Chapter Conclusion

The post-engagement phase is a time for a consultant to pull away from
a project but for the consulting company to seek out additional service
opportunities. While you will no longer communicate directly with the
client, you may be asked to contribute to your firm's efforts to provide
add-on services for the client. Most significantly, any contact you do have
is different from that during the engagement. You are no longer a team
leader or a colleague. Once again, you are the outsider with a very formal business relationship. Any communication must reflect this status.
During post-engagement, you and your firm loop back around to communicate all possible services that will help your client achieve optimal
results and make constructive change.

APPENDIX A

Audience Analysis Worksheet

Situation/Product/Delivery

Before you write something engagement-critical, perform a thorough
audience analysis.

Situation

The situation you find yourself in directs and motivates you to communicate. When you evaluate a situation, pay particular attention to your client's needs as well as your own. Survey the environment surrounding your communication to determine the conditions under which you are creating it.

Value

Identify the value to the client. Put yourself in the client's place and understand what the client needs and wants from the communication.

Purpose

State your purpose. Purpose explains your motivation and the problem or change you will address.

Message

Categorize your message. Message directly relates to your tone and, in some cases, to protocols surrounding how a communication is organized.

Directive

Identify whether this has been requested or if you decided on your own to communicate it. This controls how much you include and exclude as background.

Relationship

Identify how you know the audience, formally or informally. This identified relationship drives tone, content, format, language, and delivery.

Climate and Culture

Identify the client environment and surroundings. These elements can have an impact on what you include and exclude as well as who you choose to receive your communication.

Deadline

Identify the deadline to determine the best time for your message to be read or heard. Deadline drives when you must complete the communication and the timing for communications.

Product

Once you've considered the situational elements, the actual product you'll produce becomes much clearer. You know what both your client and you need from the communication, so you're now prepared to think through what the actual communication will look like, what it will include or exclude, what it will sound like, how it will be organized, and how long it will be.

Wrapper

Decide the best format for actually wrapping the communication (letter, e-mail, freestanding report, etc.).

Content

Determine what your content should be. This will depend on the particular business matter at hand. The situation should help guide you as you construct your content.

Organization

Decide which method of organization to use. The situation, and most importantly value and purpose, contribute significantly to this decision.

Tone

Decide your tone very consciously. Reflecting on the situation should guide your tone.

Language

Choose your language deliberately. Similar to tone, the language you use is directly related to the relationship you have with the client and the climate and culture you find yourself in.

Length

Decide how long or short your communication should be. You should write as much as the situation warrants, no more or less. Just because you have a great deal of information on a topic doesn't mean you should write or present it all.

Delivery

By this point, you've defined and made preliminary decisions about the characteristics of the product. Now you can address the actual delivery mechanism you will use to communicate your message. Decide how and when to deliver your communication for best impact.

APPENDIX B

Delivery Modes by Communication Type

Consultant documentation is created, stored, and delivered according to long-standing business practices. Electronic delivery, document sharing, and collaborative editing continually changes, based on new tools and practices. Carefully evaluate options for each document type prepared during your engagement processes.

Letters and other formal correspondence with clients (examples include letters of inquiry, sales letters, short reports, and proposals)

- Formatted as formal business letters
- Delivered either on paper or as an e-mail attachment with electronic signature
- Stored electronically on consultant digital storage platform

Agreements (examples include nondisclosure agreements, contracts, and statements of work)

- Formatted as formal contractual agreements according to company standards
- Sent for preliminary review as e-mail attachments
- Delivered either as e-mail attachments or as paper documents for signatures
- Scanned and stored electronically on consultant storage platform

Project Documentation (examples include project plans, communication plans, progress reports, project presentations, investigative reports, operating procedures and instructions, and meeting minutes)

- Formatted as formal project documentation according to company standards
- Created and edited collaboratively on consultant storage platform
- Delivered throughout engagement phase as e-mail attachments or by granting direct access, rarely printed
- Stored permanently on consultant storage platform with file copies delivered to client

Notes

Chapter 1

1. Bruni (2015).
2. Weinberg (2015).

Chapter 2

1. Smith D and Smith J (2016).
2. Welch (2015).
3. Hoppe (2006).
4. Bruni (2015); Weinberg (2015).
5. Pratt (2006).
6. Piscopo (2015).
7. Nordquist (2015).

Chapter 3

1. Holmes (2013).
2. Oliu, Brusaw, and Alred (2013), p. 353.
3. Oliu, Brusaw, and Alred (2013), p. 358.
4. Oliu, Brusaw, and Alred (2013), chapter 11.
5. Welch (2015).
6. Alred, Brusaw, and Oliu (2012).
7. Holmes (2013).
8. Oliu, Brusaw, and Alred (2013), p. 324.
9. Oliu, Brusaw, and Alred (2013), p. 358.
10. Alred, Brusaw, and Oliu (2012), p. 299.

Chapter 4

1. "Post-Implementation Reviews" (2016).

References

Alred, G. J., Brusaw, C. T., & Oliu, W. E. (2012). *The business writer's handbook* (10th ed.). Boston, MA: Bedford/St. Martins.

Bruni, M. (2015, September 15). Phone interview.

Holmes, S. (2013). Developing a team vision statement. *Make a Dent Leadership*. Retrieved from http://www.makeadentleadership.com/developing-a-team-vision-statement.html

Hoppe, M.H. (2006). *Active listening: Improve your ability to listen and lead*. Greensboro, NC: Center for Creative Leadership.

Nordquist, R. (2015, July 30). What should you include in meeting minutes? *About.com*. Retrieved from http://grammar.about.com/od/mo/g/Minutes.htm

Oliu, W. E., Brusaw, C. T., & Alred, G. J. (2013). *Writing that works: Communicating effectively on the job*. (11th ed.) Boston: Bedford/St Martins.

Piscopo, M. (2015). Statement of work template. *Project Management Docs*. Retrieved from http://www.projectmanagementdocs.com/project-documents/statement-of-work.html#axzz3yhBYQ2ou

Post-Implementation Reviews: Making Sure That What You Delivered Actually Works. (2016). *Mind Tools, Ltd*. Retrieved from https://www.mindtools.com/pages/article/newPPM_74.htm

Pratt, M. K. (2006, May 22). How to write a statement of work." *Computer World*. Retrieved from http://www.computerworld.com/article/2555324/it-management/how-to-write-a-statement-of-work.html

Smith, D., & Smith, J. (2016, February 1). Personal interview.

Weinberg, H. (2015, October 20). Phone interview and email.

Welch, J. (2015, September 29). Personal interview and email.

Index

active listening, 26
add-on services sales letters, 92,
    103–106
agreements, 18
anxiety, 23
audience analysis, 8–14
    delivery, 13–14
    elements controlling, 9–14
    post-engagement, 95–97
    pre-engagement, 26–31
    product, 11–12
    responding to messages and
        queques, 9
    situation, 10–11
avoidance, 22–23

bad news messages, 72–75
business communication, iii
    audience-focused, 8–14
    during engagement environments,
        57–58
    guidelines, 9
    negative emotions and attitudes
        impacts, 21–24
    relationship development and, 1
    style and tone of, 7
business correspondence, iii
business etiquette, iii
business writings, iii, 3–7
    general assumptions, 4–6
    medium and format for, 4–6
    polished professional delivery, 3–4

client
    concerns and desires, 27–28
    engagement environments, 56–57
    expectations and assumptions,
        20–21
    negative emotions and attitudes,
        21–24
    post-engagement environment,
        94–95

pre-engagement environment,
    20–24
climate and culture, 11
communication creation process, 7–8
communication plans, 51
company templates, 20
Computerworld, 35
consultants
    business communication as, 1–3
    critical problem of, 2
    engagement environments, 55
    listening skills, 26–28
    oral communication of, 3
    post-engagement environment, 94
    pre-engagement environment, 19–20
consulting, iii
content, 13
contract, 18
correspondence and documentation,
    92–93

deadline, 11
delivery, 109
    as element of audience analysis,
        13–14
        meeting, 13–14
        physical, 13
        virtual, 13
    modes by communication type,
        111–112
directive, 10–11
documentation, 16–17, 92–93

early engagement communication,
    51–52
e-mails, iii, 2, 52
engagements, iii, 1
    audience analysis, 60–64
    communication, 50–53
        early, 51–52
        executive meetings, presentations
          and minutes, 53

investigative reports, 53
milestone, 53
project formal reports, 53
routine ongoing, 52
environments, 54–60
    client, 56–57
    communication during, 57–58
    communication tips for new
        consultants, 58–60
    consultant, 55
    positive side of, 57
    shifting from pre-engagement to,
        56–57
instructions, 75–78
phase, 49–50
sample communications, 64–89
    instructions, 75–78
    investigative reports, 83–89
    progress reports, 78–83
    project vision statements, 64–66
    routine e-mail exchanges, 66–71
    significant bad news messages,
        72–75
expectations and assumptions, 20–21

fear of change, 21–22

impatience, 23–24
investigative reports, 53
    engagement sample
        communications, 83–89

lack of understanding, 23
language, 13
length, 13
letter of inquiry, 16–17
listening skills
    consultants, 26–28

meeting delivery modes, 13
meeting minutes, 18–19, 44–47
meetings, iii, 18–19
message, 10
milestone communications, 53
mistrust, 22
multiple audiences, 24–25
multiple representatives, 25–26

NDA. *See* non-disclosure agreement
negative emotions and attitudes,
        21–24
    anxiety, 23
    avoidance, 22–23
    fear of change, 21–22
    impatience, 23–24
    lack of understanding, 23
    mistrust, 22
    resentment, 24
    skepticism, 22
non-disclosure agreement (NDA), 18

oral communication, 3, 19
organization, 13

physical delivery modes, 13
post-engagement
    audience analysis, 95–97
    communication, 92–93
    environment, 93–95
        client, 94–95
        consultants, 94
    phase, 91–92
    sample communications, 97–106
        add-on services sales letter,
            103–106
        post implementation review
            client report, 98–103
post-implementation
    presentations and reports, 93
    review (PIR) client report, 93,
        98–103
PowerPoint presentations, 3
Pratt, Mary, 35
pre-engagement
    audience analysis, 26–31
    communication, 16–19
    environment, 19–24
        clients in, 20–24
        consultants in, 19–20
    phase, 15
    sample communications, 31–47
        meeting minutes, 44–47
        project introduction
            presentation, 40–43
        sales/proposal letter, 31–35
        statement of work, 35–40

preliminary correspondence and
        documentation, 16–17
    letter of inquiry, 16–17
    product specifications, 17
    proposals, 17
    requests for information, 17
    requests for proposals, 17
    sales letter, 17
presentations, iii, 18–19
    PowerPoint, 3
product
    as element of audience analysis,
        11–12
        content, 13, 109
        language, 13, 109
        length, 13, 109
        organization, 13, 109
        tone, 13, 109
        wrapper, 12–13, 108
    specifications, 17
progress reports, 78–83
    engagement sample
        communications, 78–83
project
    completion letters, 92
    documentation, 112
    formal reports, 53
    introduction, 19, 40–43
    plan completion, 93
    plans, 18, 51
    vision statements, 52, 64–66
proposals, iii, 17
purpose, 10

relationship, 11
reports, iii
requests for information, 17
requests for proposals, 17
resentment, 24
routine e-mail exchanges, 66–71

sales/proposal letter, 17, 31–35
    add-on services, 103–106
    guidelines for writing, 32
situation, as element of audience
        analysis, 10–11
    climate and culture, 11, 108
    deadline, 11, 108
    directive, 10–11, 108
    message, 10, 107
    purpose, 10, 107
    relationship, 11, 108
    value, 10, 107
skepticism, 22
statement of work (SOW), 18, 35–40

team introduction, 51
team operating procedures, 51
tone, 13

value, 10
virtual delivery modes, 13

wooing period, 19
wrapper, 12–13
written communication, 19

CPSIA information can be obtained at www.ICGtesting.com
Printed in the USA
BVOW02s0042070616

451003BV00005B/27/P